THE
Dinosaur
SPOTTER'S GUIDE

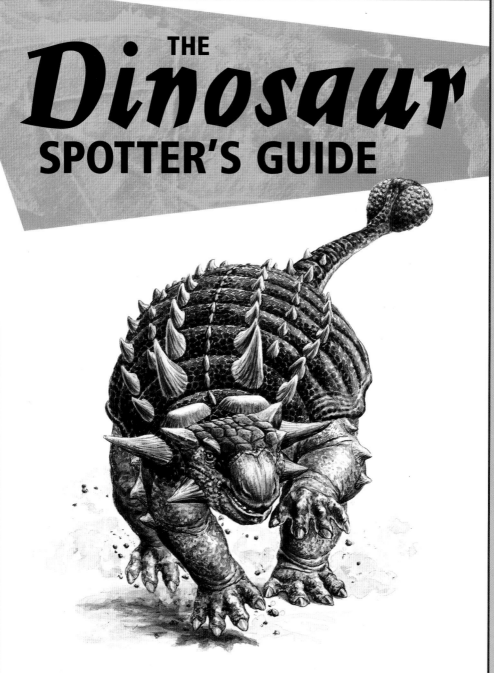

The who, when, where
of the prehistoric world

Paul Harrison

ARCTURUS

ARCTURUS

Arcturus Publishing Limited
26/27 Bickels Yard
151–153 Bermondsey Street
London SE1 3HA

Published in association with
foulsham
W. Foulsham & Co. Ltd,
The Publishing House, Bennetts Close, Cippenham,
Slough, Berkshire SL1 5AP, England

ISBN-13: 978-0-572-03259-3
ISBN-10: 0-572-03259-5

This edition printed in 2006
Copyright © 2006 Arcturus Publishing Limited

British Library Cataloguing-in-Publication Data: a catalogue record for this
book is available from the British Library

Printed in China

Author: Paul Harrison
Designers: Beatriz Waller and Linda Storey
Editor: Rebecca Gerlings

© De Agostini Picture Library: jacket; title page, contents, bottom right;
page 8; page 9; page 10, top and bottom; page 11; page 15, top and bottom;
pages 16–29; pages 32–33; pages 36–45; pages 48–53; pages 56–61;
pages 64–65; pages 70–72; pages 76–81; pages 84–87; pages 90–91;
pages 98–99; pages 102–105; pages 110–117; pages 120–125; pages 130–131;
pages 134–139; pages 142–153; page 154, bottom left; page 155, bottom
right; pages 158–159.

© Miles Kelly Publishing Ltd: contents, top right; pages 6–7; pages 12–13;
pages 30–31; pages 54–55; pages 62–63; page 92; pages 106–107;
pages 128–129; pages 140–141; page 154, top; pages 156–157.

© Natural History Museum, London: contents, top left; pages 34–35;
pages 66–67; pages 68–69; page 73; pages 82–83; pages 88–89; page 93;
pages 96–97; pages 126–127.

© Highlights for Children, Inc: page 14, bottom left; pages 46–47;
pages 74–75; pages 94–95; pages 100–101; pages 108–109; pages 118–119;
pages 132–133.

Contents

Dinosaurs

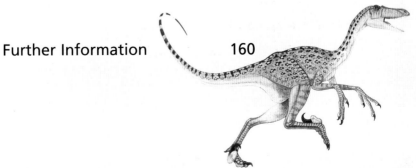

Introduction

Congratulations! You are about to embark on the journey of a lifetime; in fact, the journey of many lifetimes, as you travel back in time – as much as 245 million years – to view dinosaurs in their own habitats.

It is an unparalleled experience. These magnificent creatures ruled the earth for over 180 million years. The later dinosaurs, such as *Triceratops* and *Tyrannosaurus rex*, lived closer to our age than to many of the other dinosaurs from even the middle period of their reign.

You will discover that dinosaurs, although vastly different from the animals you may know on earth today, act in ways that will seem strangely familiar to anyone who has watched a nature documentary on television or seen animals in the wild. The way they live, eat and hunt does not look so different from how

Maiasaura and her babies

today's creatures behave. That is partly because the rules of survival 245 million years ago were exactly the same as they are today and will be tomorrow. It is also due to the fact that descendants of the dinosaurs – birds – live among us today.

This guide introduces you to the many different species you may encounter on your dinosaur-spotting trip. You will notice that the information is, at times, incomplete. Even today there are certain things that we do not know – it can be problematic, for example, to give a specific weight for some dinosaurs – so any additional information that you can discover will always be welcome.

What Is a

Although there were hundreds of different types of dinosaurs, not every animal encountered on your trip will actually be one. It is easy to forget that dinosaurs shared the planet with many other types of animals. Depending how far back you go, you will also encounter mammals, birds, insects and other land-dwelling reptiles – to say nothing of all the flying and swimming reptiles or even the fish.

Riojasaurus

Dinosaur?

Dinosaurs are a large yet very specific group of creatures. To qualify, an animal has to satisfy a number of criteria:

1 It must have lived during the Mesozoic era (see page 10).

2 It must be a reptile, although not all reptiles are dinosaurs. For example, lizards are reptiles, but they are not dinosaurs.

3 Its legs must be located below its body, giving it an erect stance, as opposed to sticking out from the sides like those of a crocodile.

4 It must have lived on land, not in the air like pterosaurs, or in the water like swimming reptiles.

Remember that not all of the dinosaurs were alive at the same time. Dinosaur species appeared and disappeared during the reign of the dinosaurs. For example, *Tyrannosaurus rex* (see page 140) never saw an *Allosaurus* or a *Stegosaurus* (see pages 24 and 128).

Nodosaurus

Time Zones

The history of the earth is divided into different times, or 'eras', each with its own name. The time when the dinosaurs were alive is called the Mesozoic era. The Mesozoic is divided into three periods, called the Triassic, Jurassic and Cretaceous.

Eoraptor –
Triassic period

The Triassic period lasted from 245 million years ago (mya) to 208 mya, the Jurassic from 208 mya to 145 mya, and the Cretaceous from 145 mya to the end of the dinosaurs (65 mya).

Ceratosaurus –
Jurassic period

The world inhabited by the dinosaurs looked vastly different from the one we know today. The countries we recognize now did not exist millions of years ago. The world is constantly changing: it always has and always will do. The land moves slowly but surely and, over time, this movement can make mountain ranges appear or whole continents vanish.

Pachycephalosaurus – **Cretaceous period**

During the Triassic period, all of the world's continents were joined together in one huge landmass which palaeontologists call Pangea. As time progressed, this block began to split so, by the Jurassic period, there were two massive continents called Laurasia and Gondwana. These in turn started to break up and, by the time of the Cretaceous period, the continents looked much like they do today.

Vegetation

The surface of the continents also looked different from the way it does today. For a start, what are now deserts – the Sahara, for example – weren't always barren sandy places, but were once rich with vegetation and vice versa.

However, most of the plants we know today simply weren't around during the Mesozoic era. There were no grasses, for instance, and flowering plants did not appear until the Cretaceous period. The main types of vegetation were ferns, cycads (palm-like trees), conifers and ginkgos (another kind of tree). But, by the end of the Cretaceous period, flowering plants were everywhere.

The temperature also changed during the Mesozoic era. During the Triassic period, it was generally warm everywhere – particularly near the centre of Pangea, which many palaeontologists believe was a desert. As the landmass broke apart, temperatures around the globe began to vary and the overall temperature dropped. Still, some estimates put the mid-Cretaceous temperatures at an average of 10°C (50°F) warmer than they are today.

and Climate

Timeline

This timeline will give you an idea of when the dinosaurs
featured in this book lived in relation to each other.
Of course, palaeontologists can't be sure whether these
dates are wholly accurate, but they are a useful guide.

Date (millions of years ago)	Dinosaur
228–220	Eoraptor
228–220	Herrerasaurus
227–220	Coelophysis
227–210	Euskelosaurus
220–210	Plateosaurus
220–210	Riojasaurus
208–190	Massospondylus
205–189	Syntarsus
200–190	Dilophosaurus
193–176	Anchisaurus
176–169	Rhoetosaurus
170–155	Megalosaurus
169–163	Xiaosaurus
157–144	Yangchuanosaurus
155–140	Brachiosaurus
155–145	Diplodocus
155–150	Kentrosaurus
155–144	Mamenchisaurus
155–144	Seismosaurus
155–147	Stegosaurus
154–147	Apatosaurus
154–135	Allosaurus
154–144	Ornitholestes
150–144	Ceratosaurus
147	Archaeopteryx
145–140	Compsognathus
140–100	Iguanodon
137–100	Wuerhosaurus

Caudipteryx

127–120	Polacanthus
126–121	Baryonyx
126–112	Hypsilophodon
125–122	Caudipteryx
120–110	Deinonychus
120–110	Utahraptor
120–111	Zephyrosaurus
117–105	Leaellynasaura
115–105	Acrocanthosaurus
112–90	Giganotosaurus
105–95	Nodosaurus
98–94	Carcharodontosaurus
98–75	Spinosaurus
90–70	Carnotaurus
85–80	Bagaceratops
85–65	Oviraptor
85–74	Protoceratops
85–80	Quaesitosaurus
84–75	Velociraptor
83–65	Styracosaurus
83–65	Tyrannosaurus rex
82–73	Maiasaura
80–75	Avimimus
80–72	Dromaeosaurus
80–70	Parasaurolophus
80–65	Troodon
79–72	Lambeosaurus
79–67	Saurolophus
79–69	Stegoceras
79–69	Struthiomimus
78–65	Albertosaurus
78–74	Chasmosaurus
78–74	Hadrosaurus
78–66	Homalocephale
78–65	Saltasaurus
76–74	Corythosaurus
76–65	Edmontosaurus
74–70	Abelisaurus
74–67	Ankylosaurus
74–70	Gallimimus
73–65	Pachycephalosaurus
70–65	Alamosaurus
70–65	Deinocheirus
69–65	Triceratops

Albertosaurus

Deinonychus

Abelisaurus

Named after Roberto Abel of the Argentinian Museum of Natural Sciences, this late Cretaceous dinosaur is something of a mystery – but we do know it's a pretty fearsome predator.

Fact File

How to say it a-BEEL-ee-SORE-us

Meaning of name Abel's lizard

Family Abelisauridae

Period Late Cretaceous

Where found Argentina

Height 2 metres (6.6 feet)

Length 9 metres (29.7 feet)

Weight 1,300 kilograms (1.4 tons)

Food Meat

Special features Not enough specimens spotted to be certain

TRIASSIC　　　JURASSIC　　　CRETACEOUS

Detective work

The problem with *Abelisaurus* is that it's an elusive character. What's more, palaeontologists have very few remains to work with; the only evidence found so far is one skull – and that's incomplete! However, even from such an unpromising start scientists can make an amazing number of assumptions about its size and what it looks like.

Hanging around

Of course, much of a palaeontologist's work is open to debate and contradiction. Many scientists are not convinced that *Abelisaurus* is a separate sort of dinosaur at all, but suspect it is actually *Carcharodontosaurus* (car-CHA-row-DON-toe-SORE-us), the big Moroccan predator. If so, it would mean *Carcharodontosaurus* was in existence not only later, but also in a different area.

Acrocanthosaurus

This Cretaceous dinosaur is a classic predator: it has a big head filled with sharp teeth, powerful legs and a big, bulky body. There is also an interesting decorative feature not normally seen on dinosaurs of this type – a frill.

Spiny

The most striking feature of this powerful dinosaur is a series of spikes running down its spine. The spikes measure around 0.4 metre (1.3 feet) in length, which is big, but probably not long enough to be useful as a form of defence. Instead, they support a frill which runs down the length of the body. But what is the purpose of this crest? If you can answer that, you're going to be a great palaeontologist because nobody is sure at the moment.

Track attack

Acrocanthosaurus is nearly as big as *Tyrannosaurus rex* and it would seem just as fearsome a predator. There are some dinosaur tracks in Texas called the Paluxy River tracks. Some palaeontologists believe that a set of these belong to *Acrocanthosaurus* and, if that's true, the tracks show it chasing *Pelorosaurus* (pe-LOH-ro-SORE-us), a type of sauropod twice the size of this predator.

Fact File

How to say it a-kroh-kan-tho-SORE-us
Meaning of name High-spine lizard
Family Carcharodontisauridae
Period Early Cretaceous
Where found North America
Height 4 metres (13.2 feet)
Length 12 metres (40 feet)
Weight 2,300 kilograms (2.5 tons)
Food Meat
Special features Crest along spine

TRIASSIC   JURASSIC   CRETACEOUS

Alamosaurus

With its long neck and whippy tail, *Alamosaurus* looks much like any other sauropod. However, it is rare because it is the only type of sauropod to be found in North America at this time.

A long way from home?

Sauropods are *the* giants of the dinosaur age. The biggest animals to have walked on land, the sauropods peak during the Jurassic period. By the late Cretaceous period, they had disappeared from North America, apart from *Alamosaurus*, who can be found in Texas, Utah and New Mexico. Some palaeontologists believe that these dinosaurs wandered up from South America, where more sauropods may still be found.

Bulky body

The largest sauropods, like *Brachiosaurus* (BRA-kee-o-SORE-us), are about 16 metres (53 feet) high and weigh over 80,000 kilograms (88 tons). Although *Alamosaurus* is much smaller, it's still big enough! Remarkably, it can even stand on its hind legs to feed on tasty leaves that might otherwise be out of reach.

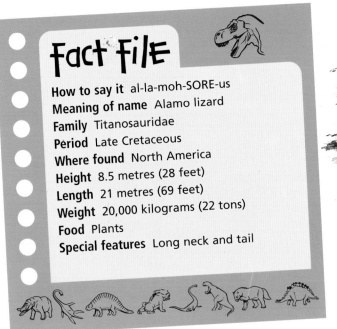

Fact File

How to say it al-la-moh-SORE-us
Meaning of name Alamo lizard
Family Titanosauridae
Period Late Cretaceous
Where found North America
Height 8.5 metres (28 feet)
Length 21 metres (69 feet)
Weight 20,000 kilograms (22 tons)
Food Plants
Special features Long neck and tail

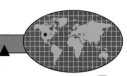

TRIASSIC   JURASSIC   CRETACEOUS

Albertosaurus

When the first *Albertosaurus* was spotted in Alberta, Canada, palaeontologists had no idea how interesting and controversial this relative of the *Tyrannosaurus rex* would prove to be.

Close family

Most palaeontologists believe that the large meat-eating dinosaurs live and hunt alone. However, *Albertosaurus* might be the exception to the rule. The remains of nine *Albertosaurus* have been found together. What's more, the dinosaurs appear to be of different ages. Does *Albertosaurus* believe that the family that hunts together stays together? This means that the other tyrannosaurs might also live in family groups, but we just haven't seen any evidence of this yet.

Fact File

How to say it al-BERT-o-SORE-us
Meaning of name Alberta lizard
Family Tyrannosauridae
Period Late Cretaceous
Where found North America
Height 3.4 metres (11 feet)
Length 9 metres (30 feet)
Weight 2,500 kilograms (2.8 tons)
Food Meat
Special features Pack hunter

Mistaken identity

A palaeontologist's job is never easy: there's now debate about exactly how many *Albertosaurus* have been found. Some albertosaurs may actually be a different dinosaur altogether – another branch of the tyrannosaur family called *Gorgosaurus* (GOR-go-SORE-us). What this proves is that the tyrannosaur family is a big one and they all have a strong family resemblance – powerful legs, short arms, a big head and scary teeth.

TRIASSIC   JURASSIC   CRETACEOUS

Allosaurus

This top-ranking predator is one of the most common and has a great range. *Allosaurus* can be found in locations as far apart as North America, Australia and Tanzania, which means that plant eaters right across the Jurassic world have plenty to worry about.

Top cat

Allosaurus is at the very top of the Jurassic food chain. For 10 million years this will be the biggest carnivore on the planet. It is more than capable of tackling most plant eaters, even up to the medium-sized sauropods. However, some palaeontologists believe that *Allosaurus* hunts in packs; a truly terrifying thought. A hungry horde of *Allosauruses* may even be capable of taking on the biggest sauropods – but the question has to be asked, would they bother when there are easier meals to be had?

TRIASSIC	JURASSIC	CRETACEOUS

Deadly cuddle

Although *Allosaurus* has relatively short arms, they are bigger and stronger than those of *Tyrannosaurus rex*, who you'll meet later. These arms are also equipped with sharp claws, which mean that *Allosaurus* can cling onto its prey while attacking its victim with savage bites.

Fact File

How to say it al-loh-SORE-us
Meaning of name Different lizard
Family Allosauridae
Period Late Jurassic
Where found North America, Australia, Tanzania
Height 5 metres (16.5 feet)
Length 12 metres (40 feet)
Weight 1,400 kilograms (1.5 tons)
Food Meat
Special features Powerful limbs and sharp claws

Anchisaurus

Anchisaurus is a prosauropod – like the sauropods but not actually related. *Anchisaurus* was one of the first of this type of dinosaur to appear in the Jurassic world, where prosauropods were the dominant plant eaters.

Body

Although *Anchisaurus* is an early prosauropod, it shares many of the features of the larger, later sauropods, which is why many people think they are related. *Anchisaurus* has a long neck and tail, a small head and stocky legs. However, unlike sauropods, it also has slender toes and odd-shaped claws at the ends of its arms. Palaeontologists think that *Anchisaurus* can stand on its back legs to reach the higher vegetation, so see if you can confirm this.

Early find

Anchisaurus remains were some of the first dinosaur bones discovered in the United States. They were found in Connecticut in 1818, although at first people thought the bones were human. Eventually, they were correctly identified and any misunderstanding was put to rest. However, some confusion remains, as *Anchisaurus* is also sometimes known as *Yaleosaurus*.

Fact File

How to say it an-kee-SORE-us
Meaning of name Near lizard
Family Anchisauridae
Period Early Jurassic
Where found North America
Height 1 metre (3.3 feet)
Length 2 metres (6.6 feet)
Weight 70 kilograms (154 pounds)
Food Plants
Special features Leaf-shaped serrated teeth

TRIASSIC   JURASSIC   CRETACEOUS

Ankylosaurus

This is the last and possibly the most famous of the ankylosaurids. *Ankylosaurus* is big, wide, heavy and covered in bony plates. This is one well-protected dinosaur, and most predators have to think twice before trying to tackle it.

Bulky

The body of *Ankylosaurus* is all about defence, being covered in thick plates of bone fused into the dinosaur's skin. This forms a hard, shell-like structure over the creature; it even has bony plates over its eyes. Not only that, but its body is covered in rows of short spikes. As if that weren't enough, *Ankylosaurus* also has a heavy, bony club at the end of its tail.

TRIASSIC	JURASSIC	CRETACEOUS

Under attack

If *Ankylosaurus* finds itself cornered in an attack, rather than run away, it will crouch low to the ground to protect its underbelly. This means the predator has to try to flip it over to get at the soft part underneath. There are two problems here: first, *Ankylosaurus* is very, very heavy, and second, the spikes on its body would make it doubly difficult to overturn. Plus, there is always the danger of getting clubbed by that dangerous tail. It could easily break a predator's leg, and a badly injured dinosaur is more than likely to end up as lunch itself for another meat eater – one more good reason for predators to find easier prey.

Food

Squat, heavy *Ankylosaurus* has little choice but to eat low-growing plants. Fortunately, this creature is not a fussy eater, as its wide mouth demonstrates, and it is happy munching on any plant that it stumbles across.

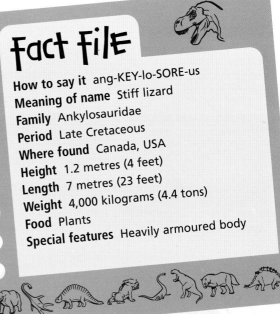

Fact File

How to say it ang-KEY-lo-SORE-us
Meaning of name Stiff lizard
Family Ankylosauridae
Period Late Cretaceous
Where found Canada, USA
Height 1.2 metres (4 feet)
Length 7 metres (23 feet)
Weight 4,000 kilograms (4.4 tons)
Food Plants
Special features Heavily armoured body

Slow but speedy

Ankylosaurus isn't the rocket scientist of the dinosaur world, having a very small brain in proportion to its body size, but then it doesn't really need to think much. However, what it lacks in brains it would seem it makes up for in speed; despite its build and short, stocky legs, some palaeontologists think *Ankylosaurus* can run quite fast (though only in short bursts).

Apatosaurus

Apatosaurus is a huge sauropod, one of the biggest types of dinosaur. Its sheer size is enough to put off most predators, and its long neck is excellent for grazing plants and leaves beyond the reach of other herbivores.

Two into one

For many years, the most complete *Apatosaurus* skeleton found was thought to belong to an entirely different dinosaur. This skeleton was called *Brontosaurus* and became one of the best-known dinosaurs. In the 1970s, it was finally proved that *Brontosaurus* and *Apatosaurus* were, in fact, the same creature. Since *Apatosaurus* had been found first, this name was used.

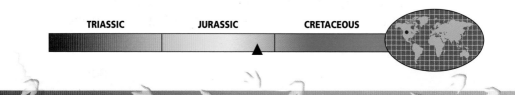

TRIASSIC	JURASSIC	CRETACEOUS

Fact File

How to say it a-PAT-oh-SORE-us
Meaning of name Deceptive lizard
Family Diplodocidae
Period Late Jurassic
Where found USA
Height 4 metres (13 feet)
Length 21 metres (69 feet)
Weight 30,000 kilograms (33 tons)
Food Plants
Special features Enormous size

Water dweller?

One unusual feature of *Apatosaurus* is that its nostrils are located on the very top of its head. In the past, this led some people to believe that it might live in water, like a hippopotamus. The idea seemed to make sense; the water would help support the dinosaur's massive body and *Apatosaurus* would be able to breathe by sticking the top of its head out of the water. Unfortunately, this interesting theory was ruined by the fact that this dinosaur has never been spotted anywhere near water; it is a land-dweller after all.

Archaeopteryx

When *Archaeopteryx* remains were first unearthed, the dinosaur was thought to be a *Compsognathus*. However, palaeontologists soon realized that this is one of the most important dinosaur discoveries ever made.

TRIASSIC	JURASSIC	CRETACEOUS

Missing link

Archaeopteryx was the first feathered dinosaur to be found anywhere. Originally, palaeontologists suggested it could be a major link between dinosaurs and birds, but now some think that *Archaeopteryx* is a bit of a dead end in avian evolution. It has feathers and light bones like birds do, but it also has a flat breastbone and a long, bony tail, which birds don't have. However, *Archaeopteryx* is some kind of link between feathered and non-feathered creatures and, as such, is a highly prized specimen.

Fact File

How to say it ar-kee-OP-ter-riks
Meaning of name Ancient wing
Family Coeluridea
Period Late Jurassic
Where found Germany
Height 0.3 metre (1 foot)
Length 0.5 metre (1.6 feet)
Weight 500 grams (18 ounces)
Food Meat
Special features Feathers

High flyer?

If you are lucky enough to spot *Archaeopteryx*, you might be able to answer a question that palaeontologists have been arguing about for years – can it fly? Some think it might be able to make extended hops by running and flapping its wings rather than actually take flight, which might be useful when chasing flying insects. What seems certain is that its feathers are used as a form of insulation, much as birds fluff up their feathers to keep out the cold.

Avimimus

You'd be doing well to spot this dinosaur because palaeontologists are still arguing about exactly what *Avimimus* looks like and what it can do!

Fact File

How to say it a-vee-MEEM-us
Meaning of name Bird mimic
Family Avimimidae
Period Late Cretaceous
Where found China, Mongolia
Height 1 metre (3.3 feet)
Length 1.5 metres (5 feet)
Weight 15 kilograms (33 pounds)
Food Meat
Special features Intelligent and speedy

Feathers

What we do know from the remains we have found is that *Avimimus* looks very bird-like with its body and beak, but there's still one unanswered question – does it have feathers? Many palaeontologists argue that it does, *Avimimus* remains have not been preserved well enough to detect such details. However, even if it did have feathers, it's unlikely that it could fly.

Quick, quick

Avimimus is quick of thought and of movement. With a light bone structure and long, thin legs, it is probably very agile. Speed would be handy since it hunts insects and lizards, which can be pretty quick themselves. It is also one of the more intelligent dinosaurs: it's brain is large for its body weight and it has very well-developed sight.

| TRIASSIC | JURASSIC | CRETACEOUS |

Bagaceratops

Bagaceratops gets its name from the short horn on its nose. The horn is a stunted version of the much bigger ones found on the larger North American ceratopids.

What it looked like

Palaeontologists consider *Bagaceratops* to be far more primitive than the ceratopids – even though it came later than many of them. Like the ceratopids, *Bagaceratops* has a relatively stocky build and short legs. However, along with its horn, its crest is nowhere near as large as those of *Styracosaurus* (sty-RAC-o-SORE-us) nor is *Bagaceratops* itself anywhere near as big. Its closest relative is probably *Protoceratops* (pro-toe-KAIR-ah-tops), which is about twice the size of its smaller cousin.

How it ate

With its beaky mouth, *Bagaceratops* has the perfect instrument for snapping off tough vegetation, but it does not have any teeth on its upper jaw, which makes chewing and swallowing the plants difficult. What it does have, however, are cheek teeth, which grind up mouthfuls of plant before they are swallowed.

Fact File

How to say it bag-a-SAIR-a-tops
Meaning of name Little horned face
Family Protoceratopsidae
Period Late Cretaceous
Where found Mongolia
Height 0.3 metre (1 foot)
Length 1 metre (3.6 feet)
Weight 3.2 kilograms (7 pounds)
Food Plants
Special features Beak and cheek teeth

TRIASSIC   JURASSIC   CRETACEOUS

Baryonyx

With a mouth packed full of sharp teeth, and with claws over 0.3 metre (1 foot) long, this large dinosaur looks like one mean customer. However, *Baryonyx* spends most of its time fishing, rather than terrifying the daylights out of other Cretaceous dinosaurs.

Gone fishin'

Baryonyx is the one of the few fish-eating dinosaurs we know of. It is perfectly designed to do this, with its long, crocodile-like snout – a perfect fish-catching tool. The other way it can help itself to lunch is by scooping fish out of the water, bear style, with a swipe of its mighty claws. These dinosaurs were believed to have eaten only fish, until the remains of a young *Iguanodon* were found inside the stomach of a dead *Baryonyx*.

Eating for England

Baryonyx was first spotted in England and was a doubly important discovery: not only was it a new type of dinosaur, it was also the first fish-eating dinosaur to be found there.

TRIASSIC	JURASSIC	CRETACEOUS

Fact File

How to say it baa-ree-ON-iks
Meaning of name Heavy claw
Family Spinosauridae
Period Early Cretaceous
Where found England, Spain
Height 2.5 metres (8 feet)
Length 10 metres (33 feet)
Weight 1,800 kilograms (2 tons)
Food Meat and fish
Special features Long snout and claws

Brachiosaurus

One of the biggest, most famous dinosaurs of all time, *Brachiosaurus* is a true giant of the Jurassic world.

TRIASSIC	JURASSIC	CRETACEOUS

Going up

Besides its very long neck, another contributing factor to the extreme height of *Brachiosaurus* is the fact that its front legs are considerably longer than its back ones. This gives *Brachiosaurus* an unusual upright stance and a marked advantage. As any giraffe knows, the youngest, juiciest shoots are often found at the top of a tree and, if you're taller than anyone else, you're going to be the one who eats them.

Pumping

Palaeontologists are puzzled how *Brachiosaurus* manages to walk around without fainting: with a head so far away from its body, getting blood to the brain must be really difficult. Does it have two hearts? Probably not, but this dinosaur must have an extremely powerful heart to get the blood all the way up there. Unfortunately, we just don't know for sure.

Fact File

How to say it BRAK-ee-oh-SORE-us
Meaning of name Arm lizard
Family Brachiosauridae
Period Late Jurassic
Where found Algeria, Portugal, Tanzania, USA
Height 16 metres (53 feet)
Length 30 metres (99 feet)
Weight 80,000 kilograms (88 tons)
Food Plants
Special features Extreme height

Carcharodontosaurus

In North Africa, there is a predator that is most definitely at the top of the food chain. With a head as big as a person, and a mouth filled with teeth 20 centimetres (8 inches) long, when *Carcharodontosaurus* takes a bite, it's a big one!

Biggest ever?

Recent sightings of *Carcharodontosaurus* have opened up an interesting debate – is this the biggest predator ever? Is it really bigger than *Tyrannosaurus rex*? The evidence seems to suggest it is actually longer, but it also looks as if it has a slighter build. So, taller but lighter? The debate rages on...

TRIASSIC   JURASSIC   CRETACEOUS

Pack of trouble

A lone *Carcharodontosaurus* is tough enough to take on practically anything it comes across – even some sauropods. It is big, muscular and fast. However, *Carcharodontosaurus* is also related to *Allosaurus*, so it's quite possible that this gigantic hunter might travel around in packs. If so, there can't be a dinosaur alive that feels safe when a pack of *Carcharodontosaurus* is on the move, so watch out if you're on their hunting grounds.

Fact File

How to say it kar-KAR-oh-don-toe-SORE-us
Meaning of name Carcharodon lizard
Family Carcharodontosauridae
Period Late Cretaceous
Where found North Africa
Height 3.6 metres (12 feet)
Length 15 metres (50 feet)
Weight 6,350 kilograms (7 tons)
Food Meat
Special features Biggest carnivore of all?

Carnotaurus

One of the stranger-looking dinosaurs, *Carnotaurus* was discovered in that fertile dino-hunting ground that is Patagonia, Argentina, home to some of the more remarkable dinosaur discoveries.

What it looked like

Carnotaurus's name tells you what it looks like and what it does. With two horns on its head, the bull bit is covered, and one look at that mouth and those sharp teeth will tell you all you need to know about what it eats. What is puzzling some paleontologists is that the jaws of *Carnotaurus* seem to be quite weak, which is an unusual feature in a meat eater.

Fact File

How to say it KAR-no-TORE-us
Meaning of name Meat-eating bull
Family Abelisauridae
Period Mid Cretaceous
Where found Argentina
Height 2 metres (6.6 feet)
Length 7.5 metres (25 feet)
Weight 1,000 kilograms (1.1 tons)
Food Meat
Special features Bull-like horns

TRIASSIC	JURASSIC	CRETACEOUS

Stumpy

Although it's a fairly rare dinosaur, we know quite a bit about *Carnotaurus*. It has pebbly skin, rather like a lizard, with bigger bumps near the spine. However, its two arms are very short – even shorter than *Tyrannosaurus rex*'s – so paleontologists aren't sure what they are used for.

Caudipteryx

China is proving to be one of the new hot spots for dinosaur watching. As new finds come to light, such as *Caudipteryx*, for example, visits to China should help our understanding of how dinosaurs developed and evolved.

Couldn't fly

Despite having feathers, *Caudipteryx* cannot fly. For a start, its arms are too short and its legs are too long. In this way, it resembles an ostrich. Also, it seems that the feathers are not the right shape for flying anyway. Again, like an ostrich, *Caudipteryx* can run pretty fast, so perhaps lack of flight isn't a problem.

Relative of birds

The shape of *Caudipteryx* is definitely that of a small therapod dinosaur, so it is distinctly different from birds. However, many features are the same. Obviously, there are the feathers, but both animals also have a wishbone – the bones are light because they are filled with air – and the feet have three forward-facing toes. Similarities like this are enough to convince most palaeontologists that birds and dinosaurs are directly related – and that *Caudipteryx* is part of that evolutionary chain.

Fact File

How to say it caw-DIP-ter-iks
Meaning of name Tail feather
Family Not known
Period Early Cretaceous
Where found China
Height 0.75 metre (2.4 feet)
Length 1 metre (3.3 feet)
Weight 7 kilograms (15.4 pounds)
Food Meat and plants
Special features Feathers

Warm- or cold-blooded?

The discovery of feathered dinosaurs opened up a hotly disputed topic – were dinosaurs warm- or cold-blooded? Today's reptiles are cold-blooded, which means that they cannot produce their own body heat. Instead, they rely on the temperature of their surroundings to feel warm or cold. But if dinosaurs can't fly, what are the feathers for? Insulation probably, which suggests that dinosaurs are warm-blooded like today's birds. The debate continues…

TRIASSIC   JURASSIC   CRETACEOUS

Ceratosaurus

The Jurassic world is certainly a dangerous place to be. Another relative of that dangerous *Allosaurus* family is the *Ceratosaurus* – a big, sharp-toothed meat eater that it is wise to stay well clear of.

Fact File

How to say it keh-RAT-oh-SORE-us
Meaning of name Horned lizard
Family Ceratosauridae
Period Late Jurassic
Where found USA
Height 4 metres (13.2 feet)
Length 6 metres (20 feet)
Weight 1,300 kilograms (1.4 tons)
Food Meat
Special features Horn on snout

TRIASSIC   JURASSIC   CRETACEOUS

Friends reunited

Ceratosaurus is a typical predator of the Jurassic period. It's big, walks on two powerful legs, and has two smaller yet comparatively strong arms with four fingers on each. As a relative of *Allosaurus*, it may even hunt in packs, an idea that might recently have been proved by the discovery of a number of different *Ceratosaurus* footprints in the same area. Of course, those footprints might also be the prints of a number of lone dinosaurs attracted by one large sauropod corpse – or maybe they all just enjoy a big group hug!

Bone head

An unusual feature of this dinosaur is the small, bony horn at the end of its nose. It is too small and blunt to be any use as a weapon, so clearly has no attacking or defensive purpose. Some palaeontologists believe that it may be used by the male *Ceratosaurus* to attract females to mate, in the same way that peacocks spread their tail feathers. But we can't prove this yet.

Chasmosaurus

This spiky dinosaur not only has the three facial horns common to dinosaurs of this type but also a series of smaller spikes running across the top of the frill at the back of its head: *Chasmosaurus* seems to be sending a powerful message to predators to keep clear.

Frills and spills

The most striking feature of *Chasmosaurus* is its huge frill. It looks more impressive than it really is – in actual fact, it's little more than a frame with skin stretched over it. This makes the frill quite weak and ineffective as a defence against attack. Palaeontologists think it might be used to impress females, or to make *Chasmosaurus* look more intimidating than it really is, or perhaps even to help regulate its body temperature.

Bone beds

Chasmosaurus remains have been discovered in so-called bone beds – areas where lots of bodies of the same species of dinosaur have been found. This evidence helps to support the theory that *Chasmosaurus* lives in large family groups.

TRIASSIC	JURASSIC	CRETACEOUS

Fact File

How to say it kaz-moe-SORE-us
Meaning of name Chasm lizard
Family Ceratopidae
Period Late Cretaceous
Where found Canada, USA
Height 2.4 metres (8 feet)
Length 7 metres (23 feet)
Weight 1,300 kilograms (1.4 tons)
Food Plants
Special features Huge frill

Coelophysis

A flash flood in New Mexico was bad news for a herd of *Coelophysis* but great news for palaeontologists. The dinosaurs were killed, but it gave scientists a fantastic opportunity to inspect their remains.

TRIASSIC JURASSIC CRETACEOUS

Light bones

Coelophysis is slight of build and, like many dinosaurs of this size and shape, it is fast – handy for both catching prey and avoiding becoming lunch for a bigger predator. The hollow bone structure of *Coelophysis*, which makes its bones very light, helps this dinosaur move even faster.

A bit of everything

Like most carnivores, *Coelophysis* probably isn't that fussy about what it eats. Its usual diet is smaller dinosaurs and mammals, fish, carrion (dead animals) and even young *Coelophysis*. We know that *Coelophysis* has these cannibalistic tendencies because a dead adult was once discovered with a baby *Coelophysis* in its stomach!

Fact File

How to say it SEE-low-FIE-sis
Meaning of name Hollow form
Family Not known
Period Late Triassic
Where found USA
Height 1.3 metres (4.3 feet)
Length 3 metres (10 feet)
Weight 30 kilograms (66 pounds)
Food Meat
Special features Light bones

Compsognathus

For many years, *Compsognathus* was the smallest dinosaur ever discovered. Not much taller than a large chicken, this little predator spends its time chasing after lizards and other small prey.

Tiny tyrannosaur?

Palaeontologists have only had the chance to study two *Compsognathus* skeletons, so our knowledge has plenty of gaps. For instance, we don't even know how many fingers it has! Evidence suggests that it only has two, much like a *Tyrannosaurus rex*. However, some palaeontologists argue that it is far more likely to have three and that the remains of the third fingers happen to have been separated from the rest of its body.

Fact File

How to say it KOMP-sog-NATH-us
Meaning of name Pretty jaw
Family Compsognathidae
Period Late Cretaceous
Where found France, Germany
Height 0.7 metre (2.3 feet)
Length 1.4 metres (4.6 feet)
Weight 3 kilograms (6.6 pounds)
Food Meat
Special features Tiny size

Bird-like

One school of thought suggests that *Compsognathus* might be covered in feathers. It is certainly quite bird-like in its build, and at one point palaeontologists wondered if it was an ancestor of *Archaeopteryx*. Unfortunately, we can't be sure at the moment – we need more sightings.

TRIASSIC   JURASSIC   CRETACEOUS

Corythosaurus

Corythosaurus is part of the hadrosaur family. Usually it walks around on two legs, but it can also drop down onto all fours when grazing vegetation.

TRIASSIC	JURASSIC	CRETACEOUS

Crest

A principal feature of some members of the hadrosaurids is the crest on top of the head. Palaeontologists are unsure of the purpose of this, but have a range of theories. It might be used simply to attract a mate, or perhaps as an aid to smell, since it seems to contain some smell receptors. However, tubes passing through the crest into the throat suggest a more interesting idea. Perhaps *Corythosaurus* uses its crest for blowing air through like a trumpet. Is this how these dinosaurs call to each other?

Duck-billed mouth

Corythosaurus is a plant eater and has a well-developed arrangement for chomping through vegetation. Like many hadrosaurs, it has what is called a duck-billed mouth, consisting of a toothless beak and a mouth filled with approximately 600 teeth. These are divided between 43 rows of teeth on the upper jaw and 37 on the lower – perfect for grinding up vegetation.

Swimmer?

When *Corythosaurus* was first discovered, palaeontologists thought it might be an excellent swimmer. It certainly has paddle-shaped hands and a slightly flattened tail, and the tubes into the crest were thought to be a kind of snorkel! Most palaeontologists now discount this swimming theory and there are no recorded sightings of this particular type of activity.

Herd animal

Corythosaurus is a herd dweller and moves in large groups in a constant search for food. Living in herds offers a degree of protection from predators, which is why so many plant eaters live in herds The best place to spot *Corythosaurus* is near swamps or shorelines because their limbs make moving around this kind of environment relatively easy, and more difficult for predators.

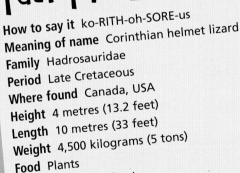

Fact File

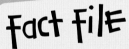

How to say it ko-RITH-oh-SORE-us
Meaning of name Corinthian helmet lizard
Family Hadrosauridae
Period Late Cretaceous
Where found Canada, USA
Height 4 metres (13.2 feet)
Length 10 metres (33 feet)
Weight 4,500 kilograms (5 tons)
Food Plants
Special features Crest

Deinocheirus

From the plains of Mongolia comes *Deinocheirus*, one of the most mysterious dinosaurs ever found. In fact, all we can give you is a vague impression of what we think it looks like.

Missing

The big problem with *Deinocheirus*, which has given rise to the great mystery surrounding it, is that so far palaeontologists have only found a few bits of backbone and its arms! But these pieces are impressive, to say the least. Each arm is about 2.5 metres (8 feet) long, ending in claws measuring roughly 25 centimetres (10 inches). Obviously, claws like that aren't just for show and make fearsome weapons, either for catching prey or for self-defence.

Fact File

How to say it DIE-no-KIRE-us
Meaning of name Terrible hand
Family Ornithomimidae
Period Late Cretaceous
Where found Mongolia
Height Not known
Length 10 metres (33 feet)
Weight Not known
Food Not known, but probably meat
Special features Large claws

TRIASSIC   JURASSIC   CRETACEOUS

Guess work

With so few remains available, palaeontologists can't really be sure what *Deinocheirus* looks like or what it can do. Some argue that it must be quite ostrich-like in build and probably one of the fastest predators around. Others point out the similarity between the claws of *Deinocheirus* and those of the modern-day sloth. Could it be that this dinosaur is an excellent tree-climber and enjoys a dangle from the branches? As with all dinosaurs, the more remains we find, the more we'll know so, until we get more evidence, an educated guess is the best we can do.

Deinonychus

Deinonychus is nowhere near the biggest carnivore on the planet, but this Cretaceous predator is one of the most fearsome. An agile and intelligent hunter, it is a fearsome dinosaur.

Gang warfare

A single *Deinonychus* would be a handful, but a whole pack would cause even the biggest dinosaurs trouble. Palaeontologists believe that these are pack hunters, gathering to attack sauropod dinosaurs such as *Tenontosaurus* – a meal that would keep a whole gang of these dinosaurs fed for quite some time.

Deadly claw

Deinonychus derives its name from the huge claw on its second toe. The claw is so large that it would get in the way when *Deinonychus* walks, unless the dinosaur can keep it pulled back: retracted from the ground, like a cocked trigger on a gun. The claw is undoubtedly a fearsome weapon, but no one has got close enough to see precisely how it's used. Palaeontologists once presumed that *Deinonychus* would slash through the flesh of its unfortunate victim, but palaeontologists now believe the claw was used to stab at the victim's arteries and windpipe instead.

Fact File

How to say it die-NON-ee-KUS
Meaning of name Terrible claw
Family Dromaeosauridae
Period Early Cretaceous
Where found USA
Height 1.5 metres (5 feet)
Length 3 metres (10 feet)
Weight 80 kilograms (176 pounds)
Food Meat
Special features Deadly claws

TRIASSIC   JURASSIC   CRETACEOUS

Dilophosaurus

Dilophosaurus is the biggest carnivore of the early Jurassic period. This long-legged meat eater is probably quite speedy and may hunt in packs.

Crest and claws

The most striking feature of this amazing predator is its double-crested head, giving it its name. These frills are probably for nothing more than display, but are impressive nonetheless.

Another unusual aspect of this dinosaur is its dewclaw – a small claw a little way up the back of each leg – similar to the dewclaws you can see on the legs of domestic dogs and cats.

Weak bite

For a large predator, *Dilophosaurus* has quite a weak bite; palaeontologists can tell this from the way the muscles are attached to the jaw. Since it can't overpower its prey with one savage bite, *Dilophosaurus* probably slashes with its sharp claws until the victim collapses from the effects of its injuries.

Fact File

How to say it die-LOF-oh-SORE-us
Meaning of name Two-ridged lizard
Family Coelophysoidae
Period Early Jurassic
Where found USA
Height 1.5 metres (5 feet)
Length 6 metres (20 feet)
Weight 450 kilograms (992 pounds)
Food Meat
Special features Deadly claws

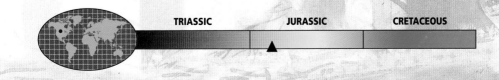

TRIASSIC   JURASSIC   CRETACEOUS

Diplodocus

One of the most famous dinosaurs of all is *Diplodocus*, a huge, but gentle and relatively slender giant. It travels in herds, constantly on the move to find new grazing areas.

Long neck and tail

The most obvious feature of *Diplodocus* is its extremely long neck and tail. Its neck is about 8 metres (26 feet) long, but at the end of it is a tiny head measuring less than 1 metre (3.3 feet). The tail is just as impressive as the neck and makes an effective whip-like weapon for repelling predators.

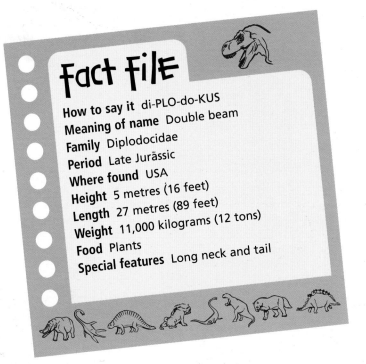

Fact File

How to say it di-PLO-do-KUS
Meaning of name Double beam
Family Diplodocidae
Period Late Jurassic
Where found USA
Height 5 metres (16 feet)
Length 27 metres (89 feet)
Weight 11,000 kilograms (12 tons)
Food Plants
Special features Long neck and tail

TRIASSIC   JURASSIC   CRETACEOUS

Ground feeder

Not all long-necked dinosaurs eat leaves from the treetops, and *Diplodocus* is a good example of this. Its front legs are shorter than its hind legs, so its neck naturally points down rather than up. The neck's extreme length allows *Diplodocus* to graze over a large area of ground without having to move.

Dromaeosaurus

Quick, agile and with keen senses of sight and smell, *Dromaeosaurus* is a highly effective predator. Despite its size, it is more than a match for most dinosaurs – especially since it works as part of a team!

Sharp teeth and claws

Dromaeosaurus has the same type of sickle-shaped claws as *Deinonychus* and *Velociraptor*, but is smaller. However, *Dromaeosaurus* does have relatively long and sharp teeth, so if the feet don't get you, the mouth will.

Balanced

All of the dromaeosaur family are agile hunters, and their tails play a big part in this. The tail is stiffened with bony rods, allowing these dinosaurs to keep them perfectly straight, which in turn helps them to stay balanced as they leap around – just like a tightrope walker holding a pole.

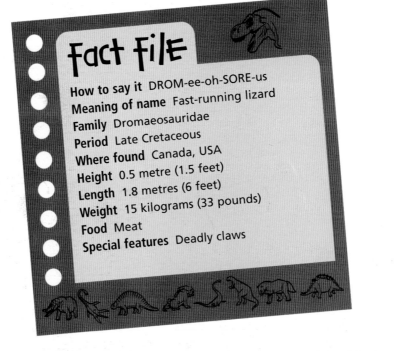

Fact File

How to say it DROM-ee-oh-SORE-us
Meaning of name Fast-running lizard
Family Dromaeosauridae
Period Late Cretaceous
Where found Canada, USA
Height 0.5 metre (1.5 feet)
Length 1.8 metres (6 feet)
Weight 15 kilograms (33 pounds)
Food Meat
Special features Deadly claws

TRIASSIC	JURASSIC	CRETACEOUS

Intelligent pack hunter

Dromaeosaurus is a pack hunter, and for a small dinosaur to be able to hunt a much larger one calls for intelligence. It would certainly seem that this dinosaur is one of the brighter ones, as it has a relatively large brain.

Beginning of the birds?

Some palaeontologists believe that birds were actually descended from small, agile predators like *Dromaeosaurus* and *Velociraptor*. Not everyone thinks so, but it does make you wonder if the *Dromaeosaurus* is feather-covered, too. Not knowing does make your chance of spotting one more difficult.

Dino hunter

The first *Dromeosaurus* was discovered in 1914 by the legendary dinosaur hunter Barnum Brown. Brown led the way in finding a many other dinosaurs, including *Tyrannosaurus rex*.

Edmontosaurus

You'll need to be in the right place at the right time to spot this Cretaceous herd dweller. *Edmontosaurus* is migratory, roaming from Alaska to Alberta to avoid the cold winter temperatures.

Puff daddy

One of the more unusual features of this particular dinosaur is its ability to inflate itself. Of course, *Edmontosaurus* can't blow its whole body up, just an area of loose skin around its nose. Presumably, the males do this as a courtship display, although it's hard to imagine what the females find attractive about their mates' ability to show off a balloon nose.

Jaw jaw

Edmontosaurus is a very efficient eater. No plant is ignored – its well-adapted jaws can chew through just about anything. They are hinged in such a way that they can move both up and down and side to side, allowing the dinosaur to grind up pretty much everything between its cheek teeth. This includes tough bits such as pine needles, which most herbivores have to leave – very handy if you spend a lot of time on the move.

TRIASSIC   JURASSIC   CRETACEOUS

Fact File

How to say it ed-MON-toe-SORE-us
Meaning of name Edmonton lizard
Family Hadrosauridae
Period Late Cretaceous
Where found Canada
Height 6 metres (20 feet)
Length 13 metres (43 feet)
Weight 3,000 kilograms (3.3 tons)
Food Plants
Special features Inflatable nose

Eoraptor

If you spot *Eoraptor* there's no point in going any further back in time, because you're at the very start of the dinosaur age!

Bad pet

Eoraptor is a small, speedy carnivore, with a light build and odd, leaf-shaped teeth. Don't get too close, however, as these teeth have a jagged edge and are very sharp. This dinosaur may only be the size of a pet dog, but it's a lot less friendly.

TRIASSIC	JURASSIC	CRETACEOUS

Is it or isn't it?

Although spotting *Eoraptor* will be exciting, there are still a number of scientists who aren't sure whether it really is a dinosaur. The problem being that there are some aspects of the skeleton of *Eoraptor*, particularly the skull, which aren't quite like that of the other, later creatures. But most palaeontologists do identify enough characteristics to classify *Eoraptor* as a dinosaur. After all, the age of the dinosaurs has to start *somewhere*.

Fact File

How to say it EE-oh-RAP-tor
Meaning of name Dawn raider
Family Not known
Period Late Triassic
Where found Argentina
Height 0.5 metre (1.7 feet)
Length 1 metre (3.3 feet)
Weight 3.5 kilograms (7.7 pounds)
Food Meat
Special features Earliest known dinosaur

Euskelosaurus

Euskelosaurus is one of the oldest dinosaurs
discovered in what is now Africa. Its similarity to some
South American dinosaurs is not surprising since, back
in the Triassic period, the continental plates
of Africa and America were joined together.

Early giant

Euskelosaurus is one of the
biggest dinosaurs you'll see in
the Triassic period. Part of the
prosauropod group, these four-
legged beasts are forerunners
of the huge sauropods of
the Jurassic period.

Herd dweller

It is quite easy to spot the
herd-dwelling *Euskelosaurus*,
often to be found
feeding
along the banks of
rivers. The herds
seem to be made
up of female
Euskelosaurus and their
young. The mothers
aren't particularly good
at child rearing – they
don't feed their young,
for example – but living
in a herd does offer a
degree of protection
for the younger,
smaller dinosaurs.

Fact File

How to say it yoo-SKEL-oh-SORE-us
Meaning of name Good leg lizard
Family Melanorosauridae
Period Late Triassic
Where found Africa
Height 3 metres (10 feet)
Length 9 metres (30 feet)
Weight 1,600 kilograms (1.8 tons)
Food Plants
Special features Long neck and tail

TRIASSIC   JURASSIC   CRETACEOUS

Gallimimus

You'll have to be quick off the mark to get a good look at one of these dinosaurs. With its long, powerful legs it is the Cretaceous equivalent of the modern-day ostrich. Some palaeontologists believe that *Gallimimus* is possibly the fastest dinosaur alive.

Fact File

How to say it gal-ee-MY-mus
Meaning of name Chicken mimic
Family Ornithomimidae
Period Late Cretaceous
Where found Mongolia
Height 3 metres (10 feet)
Length 6 metres (20 feet)
Weight 118 kilograms (260 pounds)
Food Meat, eggs
Special features Speed

Brain box

Gallimimus isn't just speedy of limb; it has a quick mind, too. This is one of the brightest dinosaurs that you'll meet, with a brain that is relatively large compared to its body size (the yardstick by which palaeontologists measure intelligence).

Beaky

Gallimimus has a very distinctive head shape, with long, toothless jaws – ideal for snapping up insects or eggs – and a small skull. It also has large eyes on the sides of its head, so it can be constantly on the lookout for predators. You can guarantee that if it spots you, *Gallimimus* will be off like a rocket, so do your best to stay hidden.

| TRIASSIC | JURASSIC | CRETACEOUS |

Giganotosaurus

When *Giganotosaurus* was first spotted in Argentina, it started a big debate – is this dinosaur the biggest meat eater ever?

Biggest of all

Many palaeontologists believe that *Giganotosaurus* is the largest of all the dinosaur carnivores – even larger than *Tyrannosaurus rex*. From sightings made so far, it certainly seems to be longer and taller than

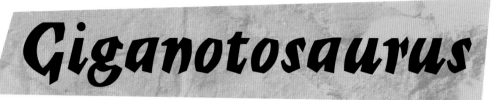

its more famous rival. However, like *Carcharodontosaurus*, it also seems to be more lightly built than *Tyrannosaurus rex*, so the argument continues about who is the king of the meat eaters.

TRIASSIC   JURASSIC   CRETACEOUS

Big appetite

It is no surprise to learn that
these giant carnivores have an
appetite to match their size, and
it certainly takes a massive meal
to keep these hunters happy.
Discoveries of titanosaurid
remains – big dinosaurs
themselves – in *Giganotosaurus*
territory suggest that even huge
herbivores were a potential meal
for this giant.

Fact File

How to say it jig-an-OH-toe-SORE-us
Meaning of name Giant southern lizard
Family Allosauridae
Period Mid Cretaceous
Where found Argentina
Height 3 metres (10 feet)
Length 13 metres (43 feet)
Weight 5,400 kilograms (6 tons)
Food Meat
Special features Biggest carnivore of all?

Hadrosaurus

One of the first dinosaurs to be spotted in the USA, studies of *Hadrosaurus* have provided much of what we know about dinosaurs today.

Herding

Like many plant eaters, *Hadrosaurus* lives in herds. Group living is a simple defence against attack from predators, and it's much easier to spot any danger lurking close by if many animals are on the lookout rather than just one.

Fact File

How to say it HA-drow-SORE-us
Meaning of name Heavy lizard
Family Hadrosauridae
Period Late Cretaceous
Where found USA
Height 3 metres (10 feet)
Length 8 metres (26 feet)
Weight 2,000 kilograms (2.2 tons)
Food Plants
Special features Paddle-like hands and tail

TRIASSIC   JURASSIC   CRETACEOUS

Swimmer

For ages, palaeontologists wondered whether dinosaurs such as *Hadrosaurus* spent most of their time in water. They have paddle-like hands and tails well suited to propelling themselves through the water. Their remains are often found beside rivers. We now know that it spends its time feeding near riverbanks but actually lives on land. However, *Hadrosaurus* is capable of swimming, so it can disappear off across the water if a predator comes too near.

Herrerasaurus

This South American predator is one of the earliest true dinosaurs, roaming the earth nearly 230 million years ago.

Early hunter

Herrerasaurus is a meat eater, as its sharp teeth clearly indicate, and it uses its speed to ambush prey. It also has long, sharp, grasping claws that are ideal for catching and tearing up meat. *Herrerasaurus* feasts on plant-eating dinosaurs and even on smaller meat eaters, too.

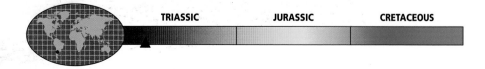

| | TRIASSIC | JURASSIC | CRETACEOUS |

Hunter or hunted?

Of course, *Herrerasaurus* won't just eat other dinosaurs. The dinosaurs do not have the planet to themselves; other reptiles and insects lived here at the same time. So, although this gives *Herrerasaurus* a wide-ranging menu, it also means that larger predators might also have put dinosaurs down as a tasty snack for themselves.

Fact File

How to say it HAIR-rare-ah-SORE-us
Meaning of name Herrera's lizard
Family Herrerasauridae
Period Early Triassic
Where found Argentina
Height 1 metre (3.3 feet)
Length 3 metres (10 feet)
Weight 75 kilograms (165 pounds)
Food Meat
Special features One of the earliest dinosaurs

Homalocephale

This unusual-looking dinosaur is a peaceful herd dweller, but you had better not get too close to its distinctive flat head because what really sets *Homalocephale* apart from the rest is its thick skull. The way its backbone is constructed seems to be designed to absorb impacts, and palaeontologists point out that the dinosaur's wide pelvis would also have been helpful in this way. But what exactly is this creature protecting itself from?

TRIASSIC   JURASSIC   CRETACEOUS

Ram bam

If, as it seems, *Homalocephale*'s head is used to withstand impact, then it must be from one of two sources – either predators or others of its kind. If the former, then it is easy to see how head butting a meat eater in the flanks might be a painful way of encouraging that predator to look for lunch elsewhere. If the flat head is for butting other *Homalocephale*, it may be used in competition for females, in much the same way that rams compete for ewes.

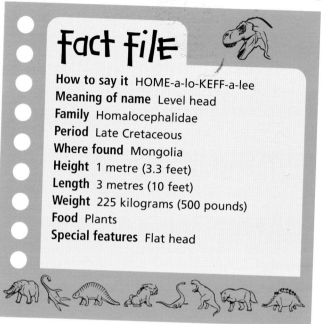

Fact File

How to say it HOME-a-lo-KEFF-a-lee
Meaning of name Level head
Family Homalocephalidae
Period Late Cretaceous
Where found Mongolia
Height 1 metre (3.3 feet)
Length 3 metres (10 feet)
Weight 225 kilograms (500 pounds)
Food Plants
Special features Flat head

Hypsilophodon

Originally, palaeontologists thought that *Hypsilophodon* could climb trees, but no one has seen this kind of behaviour yet, and most palaeontologists don't believe that they are capable of grabbing branches anyway.

Running away

Hypsilophodon may not be able to swing from branches, but it is still pretty agile. With long legs, and a tail which it stiffens for balance, this is a speedy dinosaur. Because *Hypsilophodon* is a herbivore (plant eater), this ability to change direction at speed is used as a quick getaway from predators rather than for chasing prey.

Picky eater

Hypsilophodon seems to be choosy about what it eats. Unlike the wide mouth of *Ankylosaurus*, this dinosaur has a short, horny beak, which means it can't eat just any plant it comes across. In addition to the beak, it has a series of chisel-like cheek teeth.

Fact File

How to say it HIP-sill-OFF-oh-DON
Meaning of name High-ridge tooth
Family Hypsilophodontidae
Period Early Cretaceous
Where found England
Height 1 metre (3.3 feet)
Length 2 metres (6.6 feet)
Weight 25 kilograms (55 pounds)
Food Plants
Special features Speed and agility

TRIASSIC   JURASSIC   CRETACEOUS

Iguanodon

This plant-eating herd dweller was the second dinosaur ever to be named, and it can be seen across a large part of the Northern Hemisphere.

A good sense of taste and smell

Iguanodon isn't particularly clever, but studies of its brain show it has very well-developed olfactory lobes, which are the areas of the brain that deal with smells. This means that *Iguanodon* has a good sense of smell, handy for sniffing out the tastiest plants – or a nearby predator!

Thumb spike

One unusual feature of *Iguanodon* is its thumb spike – a horny digit on each hand where you might expect the thumb to be. Palaeontologists are still divided over the function of this spike. Some claim it is for defence and can be used to stab an attacking predator. Other scientists are less sure about its effectiveness as a weapon. Maybe it is used for pulling down branches or digging up plants?

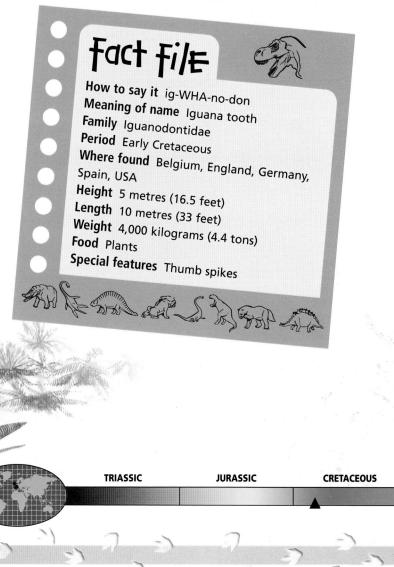

Fact File

How to say it ig-WHA-no-don
Meaning of name Iguana tooth
Family Iguanodontidae
Period Early Cretaceous
Where found Belgium, England, Germany, Spain, USA
Height 5 metres (16.5 feet)
Length 10 metres (33 feet)
Weight 4,000 kilograms (4.4 tons)
Food Plants
Special features Thumb spikes

TRIASSIC   JURASSIC   CRETACEOUS

Kentrosaurus

This unusual-looking dinosaur isn't anywhere near as ferocious as it seems. Part of the stegosaurid family, this particular species can found in eastern Africa.

Puzzling plates

Kentrosaurus has a striking combination of spikes and plates that run down its back and tail. The upper part of the back has a double row of plates; the lower portion and tail a double row of spikes. The spikes appear to be defensive but the plates are a little less easy to explain. Perhaps *Kentrosaurus* can make them change colour as part of a courtship display. Or maybe they are for regulating the dinosaur's temperature: a series of blood vessels near the surface could help cool or heat the animal.

Small brain

Famously, the stegosaurids are a bit dim and *Kentrosaurus* is no exception. But although it can't help you do a crossword puzzle, its small brain is actually quite well developed for processing smells, so *Kentrosaurus* has one good sense at least.

TRIASSIC	JURASSIC	CRETACEOUS

Fact File

How to say it KENT-row-SORE-us
Meaning of name Spiky lizard
Family Stegosauridae
Period Late Jurassic
Where found Tanzania
Height 2 metres (6.6 feet)
Length 5 metres (16.6 feet)
Weight 450 kilograms (990 pounds)
Food Plants
Special features Combination of body plates and spikes

Mismatched legs

The back legs of the *Kentrosaurus* are much longer than the front legs. This sounds odd, but it naturally points the head slightly downwards, which can be a great advantage for some plant eaters. *Kentrosaurus* is a ground feeder, browsing through low-lying vegetation, so a naturally downward-looking posture saves it having to bend down too far to eat.

Lambeosaurus

Lambeosaurus is the largest of the crested, duck-billed dinosaurs and shares many of the characteristics typical of the hadrosaurid dinosaurs.

TRIASSIC   JURASSIC   CRETACEOUS

Mixed herds

Like other species of duck-billed dinosaurs, *Lambeosaurus* is a herd dweller. Evidence shows that different species of crested dinosaurs live in close proximity to each other – much like different species of mammals are found in the same areas of savannah in Africa. Some palaeontologists believe that these different families of duck-billed dinosaurs might even migrate with one another at the same time.

Spot the difference

If group living is the norm, then these dinosaurs' crests become all the more important. Palaeontologists believe that they may be used to generate noise; however, the shape is equally important. Each species has a different-shaped crest, which is a great visual pointer for where the rest of a particular dinosaur herd happens to be – very handy if you're on the move most of the time.

Fact File

How to say it LAM-be-oh-SORE-us
Meaning of name Lambe's lizard
Family Hadrosauridae
Period Late Cretaceous
Where found Canada, USA
Height 6 metres (20 feet)
Length 12 metres (40 feet)
Weight 6,300 kilograms (7 tons)
Food Plants
Special features Head crest

Leaellynasaura

With its beaky mouth and large eyes, *Leaellynasaura* looks like many plant-eating dinosaurs. What makes this dinosaur slightly unusual is that it comes from Australia.

Fact File

How to say it LEE-ell-in-a-SORE-a
Meaning of name Leaellyn's lizard
Family Hypsilophodontidae
Period Early Cretaceous
Where found Australia
Height 0.3 metre (1 foot)
Length 1 metre (3.3 feet)
Weight Not known
Food Plants
Special features Adapted to colder, darker climates

TRIASSIC   JURASSIC   CRETACEOUS

Colder climate

Cretaceous-period Australia was attached to Antarctica, so the climate there was very different that of the present day. For the most part, the weather was cold and the days were dark. *Leaellynasaura* is adapted for those conditions – it has large eyes, which help it to see in gloomy light, for example.

Hot or cold debate

The discovery of *Leaellynasaura* reopened one of the oldest dinosaur debates – are they warm-blooded or cold-blooded? Present-day cold-blooded reptiles aren't well adapted to living in cold environments since they can't generate their own body heat. So *Leaellynasaura* can't be cold-blooded, but that doesn't mean that it is warm-blooded like mammals either – it may well be something in between. And not all dinosaurs are like *Leaellynasaura*; it may have just evolved differently.

Maiasaura

The discovery of this particular dinosaur told palaeontologists a huge amount about how some dinosaurs lived and brought up their young.

TRIASSIC	JURASSIC	CRETACEOUS

Fact File

How to say it MY-ah-SORE-ah
Meaning of name Good-mother lizard
Family Hadrosauridae
Period Late Cretaceous
Where found USA
Height 2.5 metres (8 feet)
Length 9 metres (30 feet)
Weight 3,600 kilograms (4 tons)
Food Plants
Special features Excellent parenting skills

Nesting instinct

Maiasaura is not called the 'good-mother lizard' for nothing – these dinosaurs take great care of their young. Their nests are scooped out of the ground and covered in vegetation, much like a crocodile's nest, to keep the eggs warm. When the young hatch, *Maiasaura* can be spotted bringing their babies food, and palaeontologists believe that the young will stay with their mothers for a number of years – a level of parental care uncommon in the dinosaur world.

Sociable creature

Spotting large herds of plant-eating dinosaurs is not particularly difficult. What makes *Maiasaura* special is that this species takes group living to the extreme. Herds of about 10,000 *Maiasaura* have been spotted together – young and old alike – slowly migrating in search of food or returning to their nesting sites.

Mamenchisaurus

Mamenchisaurus is yet another remarkable dinosaur from the exciting Chinese dinosaur fields and is well worth the trip for any keen dinosaur spotter.

Long neck

The most noticeable feature of this dinosaur is its amazingly long neck. At 11 metres (36 feet), it is possibly the longest of all time. The neck of *Mamenchisaurus* has 19 vertebrae, which should make it so heavy that it is difficult even to raise, never mind move. However, in this case, the bones are actually hollow and very thin – almost eggshell-thin – which allows the dinosaur complete freedom of movement.

Fact File

How to say it ma-MEN-chi-SORE-us
Meaning of name Mamenchi lizard
Family Euhelopodidae
Period Late Cretaceous
Where found China
Height 10 metres (33 feet)
Length 22 metres (73 feet)
Weight 18,000 kilograms (20 tons)
Food Plants
Special features Longest neck of all

Much like Diplodocus

Mamenchisaurus looks a lot like *Diplodocus*, especially with its long, downward-pointing neck and whippy tail. Its stance is similar, too, with longer back than front legs, giving it that familiar forward-tilted appearance. It is only when you get really close that the differences become apparent, namely the head and teeth. However, we would recommend that you take our word for it and don't venture too close yourself.

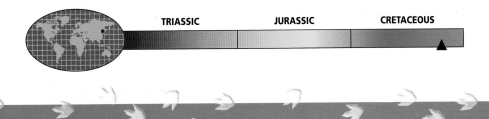

TRIASSIC   JURASSIC   CRETACEOUS

Massospondylus

Tracking down *Massospondylus* shouldn't be too difficult as they're quite common. However, just because there are a lot of them doesn't mean they're not important or interesting.

fact file

How to say it mas-oh-SPON-di-lus
Meaning of name Massive vertebra
Family Massospondylidae
Period Early Jurassic
Where found Namibia, South Africa, USA
Height 1 metre (3.3 feet)
Length 4 metres (13 feet)
Weight 1,400 kilograms (1.5 tons)
Food Plants
Special features Early plant eater

New dinosaur

Massospondylus was one of the first plant-eating dinosaurs to inhabit the planet; the very earliest dinosaurs were carnivores, such as *Eoraptor*. The meat eaters walked on two legs, so it is interesting to note that the herbivores have already reverted to walking on four. Some palaeontologists believe that *Massospondylus* can also walk on two legs if it feels like it.

TRIASSIC   JURASSIC   CRETACEOUS

Forerunner

Although *Massospondylus* is the forerunner of huge sauropods such as *Brachiosaurus*, there are differences. Size is the most obvious, plus the ability of *Massospondylus* to walk on two legs. This two-leggedness may be linked to the fact the dinosaur can grip things with its front feet and has a large thumb claw on each foot, probably used in self-defence.

Megalosaurus

In 1824, *Megalosaurus* was the first dinosaur to be named. No wonder people got excited about dinosaurs when this huge predator was unearthed!

Serrated slicers

Megalosaurus is a classic carnivore. It has powerful legs, a big head and sharp teeth that curve backwards into the mouth. Like *Tyrannosaurus rex*, the teeth are also serrated, which means they have jagged edges at the front and back.

This helps the dinosaur to cut through meat, so chomping on other Jurassic dinosaurs is no problem for this creature.

TRIASSIC	JURASSIC	CRETACEOUS

Too many to be believed

Unfortunately, when the first *Megalosaurus* remains were found they were incomplete, which meant that a lot of other partial dinosaur discoveries were thought to belong to *Megalosaurus* as well. We now know the only places to find them are England and Tanzania, so don't be fooled into looking for these dinosaurs in the wrong place.

Fact File

How to say it MEG-a-lo-SORE-us

Meaning of name Big lizard

Family Megalosauridae

Period Mid Jurassic

Where found England, Tanzania

Height 3.7 metres (12.2 feet)

Length 9 metres (30 feet)

Weight 900 kilograms (1,980 pounds)

Food Meat

Special features Rarer than first believed

Nodosaurus

This medium-sized, armoured dinosaur is quite placid if not disturbed, so it can be safely viewed from a distance.

Same but different

Nodosaurus looks a bit like *Ankylosaurus*; they're both heavy, squat dinosaurs armed with bony plates. But *Nodosaurus* is slightly different. Note how the tail has no leg-breaking club attachment and the armour lacks the spikes of *Ankylosaurus*. The mouth is different as well: it is much narrower than that of *Ankylosaurus*, which means it can't eat every plant it comes across. This armoured heavyweight feasts upon only the softer and younger plants.

Fact File

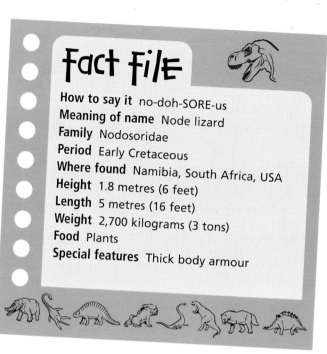

How to say it no-doh-SORE-us
Meaning of name Node lizard
Family Nodosoridae
Period Early Cretaceous
Where found Namibia, South Africa, USA
Height 1.8 metres (6 feet)
Length 5 metres (16 feet)
Weight 2,700 kilograms (3 tons)
Food Plants
Special features Thick body armour

Defensive posture

Lacking any kind of weapon, such as the lethal club of *Ankylosaurus*, *Nodosaurus* is limited in what action it can take during an attack by a predator. Not possessing the speed to run very far, it can only crouch close to the ground and wait until the meat eater tires of trying to pierce its bony plates.

TRIASSIC   JURASSIC   CRETACEOUS

Ornitholestes

A small, speedy carnivore from the Jurassic period, *Ornitholestes* is like other dinosaurs of this kind. However, our idea of what it eats is changing.

What's in a name?

Ornitholestes means 'bird eater', and it was given this name because palaeontologists believed it could eat early bird-like dinosaurs like *Archaeopteryx*. There is one problem with this theory, however – no one has spotted any of these bird-like dinosaurs in the territory of *Ornitholestes*. Either it has eaten them all already – which is unlikely – or they just can't be found here, so the name is misleading.

What it ate

If *Ornitholestes* doesn't eat birds, what does it eat? Basically, it will hunt anything small and slow enough for it to get its hands on. Its regular diet includes small lizards, mammals, insects, baby dinosaurs and even eggs if they are left unguarded for long enough.

TRIASSIC   JURASSIC   CRETACEOUS

Fact File

How to say it or-nith-oh-LESS-teez
Meaning of name Bird eater
Family Unknown
Period Late Jurassic
Where found USA
Height 1 metre (3.3 feet)
Length 2 metres (6.6 feet)
Weight 12 kilograms (26 pounds)
Food Meat
Special features Will eat most small animals

Oviraptor

This odd-looking dinosaur with a parrot-like head may have been the victim of one of the worst miscarriages of justice when it was given a name that means 'egg thief'.

Caught red-handed

Oviraptor's name seems to fit: it has a sharp beak and powerful jaws – the right tools needed for breaking eggs open. Further proof seemed to come from fossil remains, which show an *Oviraptor* crouched over some eggs, evidently in the process of stealing them. *Oviraptor* was caught bang to rights. Or was it?

Fact File

How to say it OV-ee-RAP-tor
Meaning of name Egg thief
Family Oviraptoridae
Period Late Cretaceous
Where found Mongolia
Height 1 metre (3.3 feet)
Length 1.8 metres (6 feet)
Weight 36 kilograms (80 pounds)
Food Meat and plants
Special features Incubates eggs in nests like birds

Mistaken identity

Many years later, another fossil site was found, but this time palaeontologists could see that the eggs had embryos in them – *Oviraptor* embryos. It would appear that *Oviraptor* wasn't stealing the eggs but sitting on them!

Broody

This is what you will see if you happen to spot an *Oviraptor* nest site today. Because a female *Oviraptor* does not cover her nest in vegetation like some dinosaurs, she must keep her eggs warm by sitting on them instead – just like birds do. The nests are hollowed out of the ground and can contain up to 22 eggs.

Omnivore

So, if *Oviraptor* isn't an egg thief, what does it eat? It eats both meat and plants, which is unusual for a dinosaur. It might well be tempted to eat the odd egg, too, if one comes its way. Maybe the name isn't so wrong after all.

TRIASSIC   JURASSIC   CRETACEOUS

Pachycephalosaurus

Another of the thick-skulled dinosaurs, yet *Pachycephalosaurus* is nowhere near as tough as it looks.

Not so hard

Originally, *Pachycephalosaurus* was thought to have used its thick skull to head-butt rivals in courtship displays, like some sheep do. However, a close inspection of its head reveals none of the scar tissue that head butting would cause. Some palaeontologists also claim that although the dinosaur's skull is thick, it's not actually that hard and would break under this kind of impact. In fact, *Pachycephalosaurus* uses its head to butt predators or rivals from the side, in much the same way as *Homalocephale*.

TRIASSIC	JURASSIC	CRETACEOUS

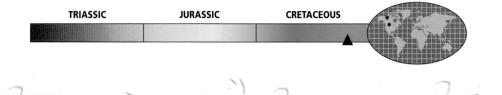

Up and down

Pachycephalosaurus might spend most of its time on two legs but, when grazing, it will happily drop down on all fours, just like kangaroos. Since these dinosaurs aren't too nippy on two legs, they will also run off on all fours when they need to make a quick getaway.

Fact File

How to say it PAK-ee-SEF-al-oh-SORE-us
Meaning of name Thick-headed lizard
Family Pachycephalosauridae
Period Late Cretaceous
Where found Canada, USA
Height 6 metres (20 feet)
Length 8 metres (26 feet)
Weight 1,800 kilograms (2 tons)
Food Plants
Special features Thick skull

Parasaurolophus

Parasaurolophus is a type of hadrosaur. Like other duck-billed dinosaurs, this peaceful, plant-eating creature uses the benefits of group living as its only defence.

Big crest

The most striking aspect of this creature is its huge crest. For a while, some palaeontologists thought it might be a snorkel, but since *Parasaurolophus* lives on land, this just doesn't add up. The horn is actually for calling out to other members of the herd. Interestingly, the male *Parasaurolophus* has a bigger crest than the female.

Fact File

How to say it par-ah-sore-ROL-oh-fus
Meaning of name Like *Saurolophus*
Family Hadrosauridae
Period Late Cretaceous
Where found Canada, USA
Height 2.8 metres (9.2 feet)
Length 10 metres (33 feet)
Weight 2,700 kilograms (3 tons)
Food Plants
Special features Long head crest

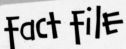

TRIASSIC   JURASSIC   CRETACEOUS

Small mouth

The crest at the back of the head is longer than the rest of the skull, which requires some special adaptations by the rest of the body. When *Parasaurolophus* needs to tip its head back, the end of the horn fits into a little dent or notch in the dinosaur's spine. If the notch wasn't there, the dinosaur would be restricted in its head movements.

Plateosaurus

Plateosaurus is one of the earliest plant-eating dinosaurs and is a forerunner – though not a direct ancestor – of huge sauropods such as *Brachiosaurus*.

Family resemblance

Like the sauropods of later times, *Plateosaurus* has thick, sturdy legs and a solid body with a long neck and tail. It also lives in herds like its distant sauropod cousins. Since this dinosaur can be spotted right across northern Europe, some palaeontologists believe that *Plateosaurus* spends its time moving from one place to another looking for food.

Distinct advantage

Although *Plateosaurus* has a long neck, which is great for reaching tall vegetation, it also has the ability to rear up on its hind legs and pull down branches with the claws on its front feet. This is a distinct advantage when reaching for the tenderest leaves at the tops of plants.

TRIASSIC   JURASSIC   CRETACEOUS

Fact File

How to say it plat-ee-o-SORE-us
Meaning of name Flat lizard
Family Plateosauridae
Period Late Triassic
Where found France, Germany, Switzerland
Height 3 metres (9.9 feet)
Length 8 metres (26 feet)
Weight 700 kilograms (1,540 pounds)
Food Plants
Special features Can rise up on its hind legs

Polacanthus

Polacanthus is another of the squat, armoured dinosaurs – this one is an early Cretaceous example from England.

Spiky personality

Like other armoured dinosaurs, *Polacanthus* uses the bony plates on its upper body and its sizeable bulk to defend itself from attack. Another distinctive line of protection is the array of spikes running down its back. These make it doubly difficult for a predator to get a grip and flip *Polacanthus* over, in order to attack the softer underbelly.

Embarrassing problem

Like *Ankylosaurus*, *Polacanthus* isn't too fussy about what it eats – and it eats a lot. And – not wishing to be indelicate – this causes a problem, especially for the dinosaur spotter, since its diet generates a lot of gas, which the dinosaur expels freely, and often. So, be warned, if you're watching herbivores like this one, don't get too close – or bring a peg for your nose.

Fact File

How to say it pol-a-KAN-thus
Meaning of name Many spines
Family Nodosauridae
Period Early Cretaceous
Where found England
Height 1.4 metres (4.6 feet)
Length 5 metres (16.5 feet)
Weight 1,000 kilograms (1.1 tons)
Food Plants
Special features Body armour and spikes

TRIASSIC   JURASSIC   CRETACEOUS

Protoceratops

We know a lot about *Protoceratops* because palaeontologists have been able to study them at every stage, from egg to adulthood.

| TRIASSIC | JURASSIC | CRETACEOUS |

Fact File

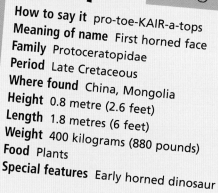

How to say it pro-toe-KAIR-a-tops
Meaning of name First horned face
Family Protoceratopidae
Period Late Cretaceous
Where found China, Mongolia
Height 0.8 metre (2.6 feet)
Length 1.8 metres (6 feet)
Weight 400 kilograms (880 pounds)
Food Plants
Special features Early horned dinosaur

Nesting

Palaeontologists know that *Protoceratops* are good parents and you can see this for yourself if you visit one of their nesting sites. The mother digs a hole in the ground before carefully laying the eggs so they point outwards. After the eggs hatch, the adults stand guard to protect the young from predators as best they can.

Threat

Protoceratops was one of the early horned dinosaurs, although actually its horn is little more than a bump on its nose. About the size of a sheep or a pig, and not a particularly fast mover, this dinosaur is prey to carnivores such as *Velociraptor*. *Protoceratops* live in herds for protection.

Quaesitosaurus

This long-necked sauropod moves in herds across Mongolia. Like its cousin, *Diplodocus*, it has a whip-like tail that it uses as a weapon against predators.

Massive muncher

Quaesitosaurus, like all the large sauropods, has to consume a huge amount of food every day just to keep going. For a big dinosaur, it has only got a little mouth, so those jaws work hard every day, especially seeing as leaves are not always the most nutritious of foods. These dinosaurs spend most of their time eating.

TRIASSIC	JURASSIC	CRETACEOUS

Stomach stones

Many plant-eating dinosaurs
– *Quaesitosaurus* included –
carry gastroliths in their
stomachs. These are stones
that the dinosaur swallows
to help grind up the food
inside its stomach. Some
birds, such as chickens,
do this, too.

Fact File

How to say it kway-zee-toe-SORE-us
Meaning of name Abnormal lizard
Family Diplodocidae
Period Late Cretaceous
Where found Mongolia
Height 7.6 metres (25 feet)
Length 20 metres (66 feet)
Weight Not known
Food Plants
Special features Whip-like tail

Rhoetosaurus

Rhoetosaurus looks like a classic sauropod with its long neck and tail and a large body supported by big, thick legs. But this one is a little bit special.

Two good reasons

Tracking down *Rhoetosaurus* is worth the effort since it is a very early example of a sauropod, dating from the mid-Jurassic period. It's also the largest dinosaur found in Australia. Most Australian dinosaurs are spotted in the area that is now Queensland, so that would be the best place to look.

Sting in the tail?

Rhoetosaurus is a rare old dinosaur and palaeontologists haven't had a chance to study it properly yet. They're not even really sure what its tail looks like. We do, however, know it's a whip-like tail, but some scientists believe it has spikes on the end, too. That would be a formidable weapon.

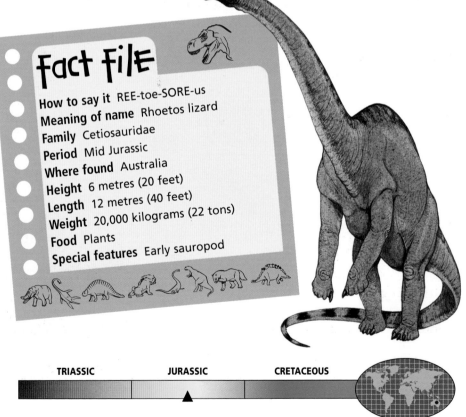

Fact File

How to say it REE-toe-SORE-us
Meaning of name Rhoetos lizard
Family Cetiosauridae
Period Mid Jurassic
Where found Australia
Height 6 metres (20 feet)
Length 12 metres (40 feet)
Weight 20,000 kilograms (22 tons)
Food Plants
Special features Early sauropod

TRIASSIC	JURASSIC	CRETACEOUS

Riojasaurus

If you're spotting dinosaurs in Argentina be sure to look out for this placid plant eater – and, at this size, it shouldn't be too difficult to find.

Getting bigger

This creature is a good example of how plant eaters continue to get bigger and bigger as the reign of the dinosaurs goes on. Food is plentiful, and their size enables the larger dinosaur to reach taller vegetation. Size also brings a measure of protection: *Riojasaurus* is just too difficult a proposition for most carnivores to take on.

Early giant

Riojasaurus is another huge dinosaur from the late Triassic period. This makes it one of the earliest large herbivores. Although not directly related to the massive sauropods of the Jurassic and Cretaceous ages, it can still match some of them in size and bulk. However, unlike some of the sauropods, *Riojasaurus* cannot stand up on its hind legs.

Fact File

How to say it REE-o-ha-SORE-us
Meaning of name Rioja lizard
Family Melanorosauridae
Period Late Triassic
Where found Argentina
Height 5 metres (16.5 feet)
Length 11 metres (36 feet)
Weight Not known
Food Plants
Special features Big for its time

TRIASSIC	JURASSIC	CRETACEOUS

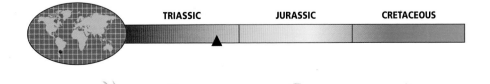

Saltasaurus

The range of dinosaurs spotted in Argentina is very different from that on other continents. *Saltasaurus* is a good example – Argentina promises to hold a wide range of sauropods.

TRIASSIC	JURASSIC	CRETACEOUS

Fact File

How to say it salt-a-SORE-us
Meaning of name Salta lizard
Family Titanosauridae
Period Late Cretaceous
Where found Argentina, Uruguay
Height 5 metres (16.5 feet)
Length 12 metres (40 feet)
Weight 7,000 kilograms (7.7 tons)
Food Plants
Special features Armour plating

Protective mothers

If you are lucky, you may encounter a herd of these dinosaurs at their nesting site. Here they will dig holes in the earth and lay their eggs. The eggs are buried in soil for incubation and, when they have hatched, the adult *Saltasaurus* will protect their young from any predators who approach in the hope of finding an easy meal.

Something extra

Saltasaurus is much like any other sauropod: a long neck and tail, small head, big body and so on. But it has something else as well – armour plating. Its back is covered with small, bony plates and bumps and, while these are in no way as protective as the armour of *Ankylosaurus*, they are still a useful defence against attack. Since *Saltasaurus* is one of the smaller sauropods, any extra protection has to be welcome.

Saurolophus

Duck-billed dinosaurs such as *Saurolophus* are very common, but if you want to see how dinosaurs operate as a herd, then watching the various members of the hadrosaur family is a rewarding experience.

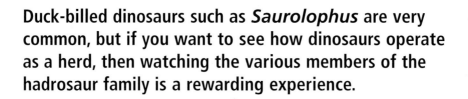

Noisy place

As with other hadrosaurs, the crest of *Saurolophus* is used as a communication device. In this instance, tubes from within the crest link up to a balloon-like pouch on the creature's snout. Because *Saurolophus* travel in herds, they can be noisy company to keep.

TRIASSIC	JURASSIC	CRETACEOUS

fact file

How to say it SORE-OL-o-fus
Meaning of name Ridged lizard
Family Hadrosauridae
Period Late Cretaceous
Where found Canada, Mongolia
Height 4 metres (13.2 feet)
Length 9 metres (30 feet)
Weight 1,800 kilograms (2 tons)
Food Plants
Special features Nose pouch

Mastication

Because *Saurolophus* is a duck-billed dinosaur, it does not have any front teeth. It has hundreds of teeth further back within its jaws instead. These cheek teeth are excellent for grinding the plants that the dinosaur pulls up, making the whole process of digesting them easier.

Seismosaurus

Seismosaurus is a real record breaker, since many palaeontologists believe that it is the longest of all dinosaurs. It is a great specimin to spot, but don't get too close to that whip-like tail.

Short legs

Seismosaurus might be the longest dinosaur, but it's not the tallest by any means, because of its relatively short legs. These little legs – and the front ones are shorter than the back – might help to make *Seismosaurus* a little more stable. That can only be a good thing since you wouldn't want one of these creatures falling on you.

Longest of all

At around 40 metres (110 feet) this is a very long dinosaur indeed, as long as about nine family cars parked end to end, or half the length of a football pitch. This makes *Seismosaurus* the longest animal to have ever lived. When a herd of these giants are on the move, you can guarantee that the front of the group will be a long way ahead of the back.

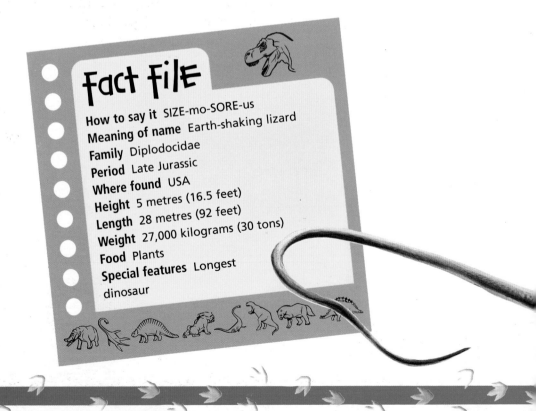

Fact File

How to say it SIZE-mo-SORE-us
Meaning of name Earth-shaking lizard
Family Diplodocidae
Period Late Jurassic
Where found USA
Height 5 metres (16.5 feet)
Length 28 metres (92 feet)
Weight 27,000 kilograms (30 tons)
Food Plants
Special features Longest dinosaur

Too big for forests

Like its cousin, *Diplodocus*, *Seismosaurus* has a long neck. In addition to allowing it to graze over a large area without moving, it also allows the dinosaur to nose around places its bulky body prevents it from going, such as in between trees.

Peg-like teeth

Seismosaurus has peg-like teeth, like *Diplodocus*. These are ideal for stripping vegetation from trees or low-lying shrubs but they're not so good for chewing up food. As a result, *Seismosaurus* swallows the leaves and stems more or less whole.

TRIASSIC   JURASSIC   CRETACEOUS

Spinosaurus

This dinosaur might look a bit odd, but you wouldn't want to say that to its face – this late Cretaceous predator is even longer than *Giganotosaurus*.

Sail

The most striking feature of *Spinosaurus* is the huge sail on its back. This isn't for any kind of defensive purpose – a meat eater like this has little to fear – instead, it is used to regulate the dinosaur's temperature. Blood is pumped around the sail, where it is either heated in the sun or cooled in the shade; this, in turn, controls the temperature of *Spinosaurus*. Although sails are relatively rare feature, they can be found on other dinosaurs and on reptiles, such as *Dimetrodon*, which were around even earlier than the dinosaurs.

TRIASSIC	JURASSIC	CRETACEOUS

Fact File

How to say it SPINE-o-SORE-us
Meaning of name Thorn lizard
Family Spinosauridae
Period Late Cretaceous
Where found Egypt, Morocco
Height 5 metres (16.5 feet)
Length 16 metres (53 feet)
Weight 3,600 kilograms (4 tons)
Food Meat
Special features Large sail

Something fishy

The best place to spot *Spinosaurus* is along the water's edge since, like *Baryonyx*, *Spinosaurus* is a fish-eating dinosaur. The advantages of eating fish are obvious: because there are few dinosaurs with a taste for fish, *Spinosaurus* has therefore always had a big supply to hand.
Of course, when it fancies a change, *Spinosaurus* will snap up anything else that comes within reach.

Stegoceras

Stegoceras is about the size of a large sheep and is the smallest member of the **Pachycephalosaurus** family. However, it shares all of the same features – in particular, the controversial thick skull.

Growing pains

Like the other members of its family, *Stegoceras* were thought to head-butt each other in a mating display, but now this appears not to be the case. Palaeontologists have looked at the remains of *Stegoceras* skulls and discovered soft tissue. In the past, this was thought to absorb the impact of blows, but now we know that it is, in fact, a sign of bone growth – the remains being investigated were from young *Stegoceras*! Older ones don't have this softer material.

TRIASSIC	JURASSIC	CRETACEOUS

Fact File

How to say it STEG-o-ser-as
Meaning of name Horny roof
Family Pachycephalosauridae
Period Late Cretaceous
Where found Canada, USA
Height 5 metres (16.5 feet)
Length 1.2 metres (4 feet)
Weight 78 kilograms (172 pounds)
Food Plants
Special features Thick skull

Rooster booster

Stegoceras sightings are few and far between so, if you do spot one, you may be able to give a definitive answer to one question: do adult male *Stegoceras* have a crest on their heads like cockerels do?

Stegosaurus

Stegosaurus is the largest member of the stegosaur family – a wide-ranging group of large plant-eating dinosaurs found around the world.

Pointless plates?

The most impressive features of *Stegosaurus* are undoubtedly the two rows of plates running down its back. When these were first spotted, palaeontologists presumed they were for defence; we now know this isn't the case. Firstly, the plates are too weak to hold off another dinosaur. Secondly, they don't really protect the most vulnerable parts of the dinosaur, such as its belly region.

TRIASSIC   JURASSIC   CRETACEOUS

Cool

So, if the plates don't protect the dinosaur, what do they do? Our best guess is that they are used to regulate the temperature of *Stegosaurus* in a similar way to the crest of *Spinosaurus*. Another theory is that they might be used in courtship displays.

fact file

How to say it STE-go-SORE-us
Meaning of name Roof lizard
Family Stegosauridae
Period Late Jurassic
Where found USA
Height 2.8 metres (9 feet)
Length 9 metres (30 feet)
Weight 2,700 kilograms (3 tons)
Food Plants
Special features Double row of plates

Defence

Just because the plates don't offer much in the way of protection doesn't mean that *Stegosaurus* has no defence against attack. Its tail is armed with four fearsome spikes, and you can bet a dinosaur of this size could inflict a mighty thrashing on any foe.

Struthiomimus

Take care when watching *Struthiomimus* – if it is scared, it will be off like a rocket and you'll stand little chance of catching it.

Super-speedy

Struthiomimus is one of the fastest dinosaurs. Built like an ostrich, with two long, powerful legs, this speedy dinosaur can nip along at about 64 kilometres per hour (or about 38 miles per hour), more than fast enough to escape from any predator.

Quick turn

Flat-out speed isn't all that *Struthiomimus* has to rely on – it's also pretty agile. Its tail is stiffened, which gives it great balance, allowing the dinosaur to turn sharply and at speed – perfect for eluding the more lumbering meat eaters.

Toothless

Struthiomimus doesn't have any teeth, but that doesn't prevent it from enjoying a varied diet. It likes to snack on anything, from small insects to eggs and even plants and fruits.

Fact File

How to say it STRUTH-ee-om-MEEM-us
Meaning of name Ostrich mimic
Family Ornithomimidae
Period Late Cretaceous
Where found USA
Height 2 metres (6 feet)
Length 4 metres (13 feet)
Weight 150 kilograms (330 pounds)
Food Meat and plants
Special features Extreme speed

TRIASSIC	JURASSIC	CRETACEOUS

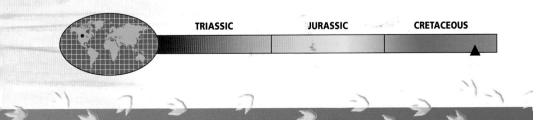

Styracosaurus

Despite its fearsome appearance, *Styracosaurus* is a peaceful dinosaur, like all members of the ceratopsid family. It lives in small herds and eats plants, migrating slowly across the continent in search of food.

Show-off

Those spiky horns on the edge of the head of *Styracosaurus* might look dangerous, but many palaeontologists believe they are just for show. The pointy frill makes the dinosaur appear even bigger and more threatening than it really is. The frills may sometimes be brightly coloured, too, to create a really impressive display.

Straight to the point

The frills may be for show, but the horn of *Styracosaurus* is the real deal. At about 0.6 metre (2 feet) long, it makes a formidable weapon. As if the horn isn't enough of a threat, *Styracosaurus* has another important weapon in its armoury – teamwork. When a predator approaches, the herd closes together in a circle, with the young safely in the middle while the adults present a wall of horns to the oncoming foe.

Fact File

How to say it sty-RAC-o-SORE-us
Meaning of name Spiked lizard
Family Ceratopsid
Period Late Cretaceous
Where found Alberta and Montana, USA
Height 1.8 metres (6 feet)
Length 5 metres (16.5 feet)
Weight 1,450 kilograms (1.6 tons)
Food Plants
Special features Large, spiked frill and sharp horn on its nose

TRIASSIC   JURASSIC   CRETACEOUS

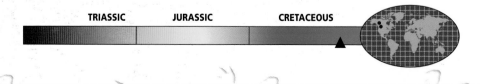

Syntarsus

Syntarsus is one of the first meat-eating dinosaurs to have appeared in the Jurassic period. It is a small dinosaur that can run quickly, thanks to its light build. Palaeontologists believe that the female *Syntarsus* is larger than the male and a lot more common.

Same but different

Syntarsus is found in both America and Africa, which supports the idea that these two continents were once joined. When they separated, *Syntarsus* began to evolve slightly differently. The American *Syntarsus* grew a pair of small crests on the top of its head – a flashy feature missing from the African variety.

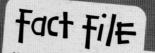

Fact File

How to say it sin-TAR-sus
Meaning of name Fused ankle
Family Ceratosaur
Period Early Jurassic
Where found USA, Africa
Height 0.8 metre (2.6 feet)
Length 3 metres (10 feet)
Weight 23 kilograms (51 pounds)
Food Meat
Special features Fast runner

One of the gang

Although *Syntarsus* is small and lightly built, it is an effective predator. Much like wolves, *Syntarsus* hunt in packs, so these dinosaurs are very good at tackling much larger animals. However, they are not fussy eaters, and are just as happy feeding on small mammals or scavenging for dead animals.

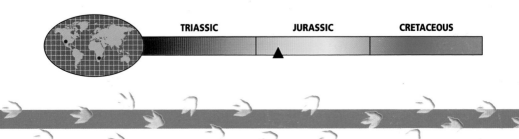

TRIASSIC   JURASSIC   CRETACEOUS

Triceratops

One of the most famous dinosaurs you'll ever see, this big bruiser of a plant eater is one of the most common Cretaceous dinosaurs.

Pointy

Triceratops is famous for the three sharp horns on its head, which give it its name. Partly for display but mainly for defence, these three prongs are equally effective in scaring off carnivores (and male love rivals) as they are attracting females. The formidable horns, particularly the pair of metre-long upper horns, are more than sharp enough to kill anything in their way – which is why all but the biggest or smartest carnivores are tempted to give *Triceratops* a wide berth.

TRIASSIC   JURASSIC   CRETACEOUS

Fact File

How to say it tri-SER-ra-tops
Meaning of name Three-horned face
Family Ceratopidae
Period Late Cretaceous
Where found USA
Height 3 metres (10 feet)
Length 9 metres (30 feet)
Weight 5,400 kilograms (6 tons)
Food Plants
Special features Horns and frill

Frilly

Of course, the horns are only effective if *Triceratops* is facing its foe. What happens if it is attacked from behind? If a meat eater tried to grab *Triceratops* around the neck – as lions do to their prey – then its huge, bony crest should stop its attacker achieving a clean bite long enough – with any luck – for the *Triceratops* to shake it off.

Troodon

This agile hunter has sharp claws on both its hands and feet and is happy to prey on anything small and slow enough for it to catch.

Dentist's delight

Although *Troodon*'s prey might disagree, the thing which palaeontologists find particularly exciting about *Troodon* are its teeth. Almost triangular in shape, they have spiky edges on both sides, making them incredibly sharp. *Troodon* also has a large number of them – some palaeontologists estimate that it has over 100 teeth – so, if anything ends up in its mouth, you can be fairly sure it's going to stay there.

Fact File

How to say it TROH-o-don
Meaning of name Wounding tooth
Family Troodontidae
Period Late Cretaceous
Where found USA
Height 1 metre (3.3 feet)
Length 2 metres (6.6 feet)
Weight 45 kilograms (99 pounds)
Food Meat
Special features Good eyesight and lots of teeth

TRIASSIC　　JURASSIC　　CRETACEOUS

Mastermind

Troodon is possibly the brightest of all dinosaurs. Its brain is the largest in relation to its body weight, the measure palaeontologists use to determine intelligence. It also has large eyes, which indicates good sight and the fact that it can probably see well even as dusk begins to fall. These abilities, combined with its speed, make *Troodon* a very competent hunter.

Tyrannosaurus Rex

Without a doubt, the most famous species of dinosaur is *Tyrannosaurus rex*. First discovered by Barnum Brown in 1902, this immense meat-eating dinosaur soon captured the public imagination. However, even though we have been studying it for over 100 years, there are still plenty of things we don't know about *Tyrannosaurus rex*.

Was he the king?

Until recently, *Tyrannosaurus rex* was the undisputed king of dinosaurs. It was thought to be bigger and meaner than any other dinosaur. But in the 1990s, two discoveries threatened to topple the king. *Carcharodontosaurus*, discovered in Morocco, and *Giganotosaurus*, from Argentina, (see pages 42 and 74), might actually be bigger than *Tyrannosaurus rex*!

Little arms

The question which has been puzzling palaeontologists longer than any other is what are those tiny front arms for? They don't reach the mouth of the *Tyrannosaurus*, and the two claws at the end make them pretty useless for gripping. Compared to the dinosaur's powerful legs and jaws, the arms look feeble. They have to be there for a reason – we just don't know what … yet.

The banana bites back

The mouth of the *Tyrannosaurus rex* is filled with over 60 razor-sharp teeth. They are as long as a banana and are curved, too, bending backwards into the dinosaur's mouth. This odd shape means that when a *Tyrannosaurus* bites into its prey, it is even harder for the unfortunate creature to escape. The *Tyrannosaurus* also has extremely powerful jaw muscles – strong enough to break even the thickest bones of its prey.

Hunter or scavenger?

One of the great debates in the dinosaur world is whether *Tyrannosaurus rex* is the ferocious predator we always imagined it to be or a sneaky scavenger looking for dead animals to eat. People who believe it is a scavenger point out that tyrannosaurs probably aren't fast enough to catch most dinosaurs. The idea that *Tyrannosaurus* is a hunter comes from its strong skull bones and sturdy build – exactly what the dinosaur needs to attack other animals.

Fact File

How to say it tie-RAN-o-SORE-us
Meaning of name Tyrant lizard king
Family Tyrannosaur
Period Late Cretaceous
Where found North America
Height 4 metres (13.2 feet)
Length 14 metres (46 feet)
Weight 7,000 kilograms (7.7 tons)
Food Meat
Special features Large, sharp teeth and powerful jaws

TRIASSIC   JURASSIC   CRETACEOUS

Utahraptor

Utahraptor is a dromaeosaurid and, like its relatives, it is an agile and intelligent hunter. It also has the stiffened tail that helps it to balance when it attacks using its deadly claws.

Big hunter

Utahraptor is the largest member of the dromaeosaurids – almost twice the size of its more famous relative, *Velociraptor* (vel-OSS-ee-rap-tor). Like its smaller cousins, *Utahraptor* hunts in packs – a truly terrifying prospect, since a group of these hunters are more than capable of taking down all but the very biggest dinosaurs.

Fact File

How to say it YOO-ta-RAP-tor
Meaning of name Utah raider
Family Dromaeosauridae
Period Early Cretaceous
Where found USA
Height 3 metres (9.9 feet)
Length 6 metres (19.8 feet)
Weight 1,000 kilograms (1.1 tons)
Food Meat
Special features Deadly claw on each foot

TRIASSIC	JURASSIC	CRETACEOUS

Teeth and claws

Like the rest of the raptor family, *Utahraptor* has a large sickle-shaped claw – over 30 centimetres (almost 1 foot) – on each foot, which it uses to stab its prey. A single blow to the windpipe is enough to kill another animal. *Utahraptor* also has a series of sharp teeth, which like those of many predators, are serrated to ease cutting through flesh.

Velociraptor

Velociraptor is one of the most famous dinosaurs around and easily the best known of the dromaeosaurids. Although not the largest of predators, its keen intelligence and teamwork ensure that it never goes hungry for long.

Hooked and chewed

Although *Velociraptor*'s claw is primarily a stabbing weapon, it can also be used to attach the dinosaur to its prey. With smaller prey, a *Velociraptor* claw can puncture an artery or windpipe. With larger dinosaurs, it's a bit trickier. The *Velociraptor* team must jump on their victim and cling on with their long claws while they chew with their teeth and scratch with their hands, until the unfortunate prey collapses and dies.

TRIASSIC	JURASSIC	CRETACEOUS

Fact File

How to say it vel-OSS-ee-rap-tor
Meaning of name Speedy raider
Family Dromaeosauridae
Period Late Cretaceous
Where found Mongolia
Height 1 metre (3.3 feet)
Length 2 metres (6.6 feet)
Weight 15 kilograms (33 pounds)
Food Meat
Special features Intelligence and deadly claws

Cannibalistic?

Although *Velociraptor* can usually be found attacking *Protoceratops* and hadrosaurs, it has been known to kill a more surprising species – its own. Remains of one *Velociraptor* skull clearly show that it had been pierced by another *Velociraptor* claw. Did an argument get out of hand? Was it mating rivalry? Or does *Velociraptor* prey on its own kind, perhaps old or sick individuals? After all, a meal's a meal.

Wuerhosaurus

Wuerhosaurus is a Chinese member of the stegosaur family – one of the latest examples – however, with lower, more rounded plates than its older relatives.

A bit slow

In common with other stegosaurids, *Wuerhosaurus* has one of the smallest brains in relation to its body size – the measure palaeontologists use to gauge intelligence. So basically, you can assume that they are a bit on the thick side – in fact, possibly the least intelligent of all the dinosaurs. But then again, how bright do you have to be to eat leaves all day?

Thagomizer

Like its more famous cousin, *Stegosaurus*, *Wuerhosaurus* has a fearsome weapon at the end of its tail. These four sharp spikes are quite effective at warding off all but the biggest or most persistent of predators. The name palaeontologists use for the stegosaurid club is 'thagomizer', which comes from a Gary Larson cartoon showing a caveman telling others that the pointy end of a *Stegosaurus* was named after the late Thag Simmons, who was apparently killed by a thagomizer.

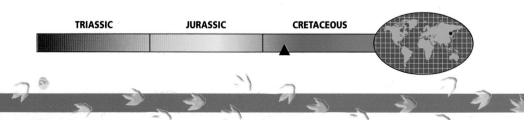

TRIASSIC   JURASSIC   CRETACEOUS

Fact File

How to say it WER-oh-SORE-us
Meaning of name Wuerho lizard
Family Stegosauridae
Period Early Cretaceous
Where found China
Height 2 metres (6.6 feet)
Length 8 metres (26 feet)
Weight 3,600 kilograms (4 tons)
Food Plants
Special features Double row of plates and spiked tail

Xiaosaurus

Xiaosaurus is another discovery from one of the newest and most exciting dinosaur sites – China. This country appears to have a large and diverse range of dinosaurs, so it's definitely worth a visit.

Mystery dinosaur

One of the rarest dinosaurs ever discovered, *Xiaosaurus* is something of a mystery. We know so little about it that palaeontologists can't even say which family it's from. We do know, however, that *Xiaosaurus* is a small, two-legged, or bi-pedal, dinosaur. We also know it's a plant eater and from what we have seen, palaeontologists believe it might live in family groups.

Fact File

How to say it zoo-SORE-us
Meaning of name Small lizard
Family Not known
Period Mid Jurassic
Where found China
Height 0.5 metre (1.7 feet)
Length 1 metre (3.3 feet)
Weight 7 kilograms (15.4 pounds)
Food Plants
Special features Too rare to define

TRIASSIC	JURASSIC	CRETACEOUS

Hide-and-seek

The biggest problem for the dinosaur spotter is that *Xiaosaurus* is very hard to find. It lives in the Jurassic forest, where the dinosaur's small size and alert nature allows it to disappear into the shadows whenever it feels threatened. In time, we might know more about this agile little herbivore but, right now, gaps remain in our knowledge.

Yangchuanosaurus

With so many plant eaters being spotted in China, it will come as no surprise that there are some ferocious meat eaters around too, looking for lunch. And *Yangchuanosaurus* is just such a dinosaur.

Toothy terror

Yangchuanosaurus is a member of the allosaurid family. It is slightly smaller than *Allosaurus*, but has more teeth. Like most classic large predators, *Yangchuanosaurus* has two strong legs, smaller arms, and a large head. It is big enough to prey on most of the plant eaters of the period – and other meat eaters for that matter – including some sauropods.

Fact File

How to say it YANG-chew-an-oh-SORE-us
Meaning of name Yangchuan lizard
Family Sinraptoridae
Period Late Jurassic
Where found China
Height 4.6 metres (15 feet)
Length 10 metres (33 feet)
Weight 3,100 kilograms (3.5 tons)
Food Meat
Special features Numerous teeth

TRIASSIC   JURASSIC   CRETACEOUS

Another show-off

No one has spotted one yet, but some palaeontologists think that *Yangchuanosaurus* might have a head crest – maybe only the males. This crest could be used in courtship displays, much like a peacock's tail, or to intimidate male rivals.

Zephyrosaurus

Not many dinosaurs begin with the letter Z, so *Zephyrosaurus* is something of a collector's item. Keep your eyes peeled for this one if you're spotting in the United States.

Fact File

How to say it ZEFF-ear-row-SORE-us
Meaning of name Zephyr's lizard
Family Hypsilophodontidae
Period Early Cretaceous
Where found USA
Height 1 metre (3 feet)
Length 2 metres (6 feet)
Weight Not known
Food Plants
Special features Agile

TRIASSIC   JURASSIC   CRETACEOUS

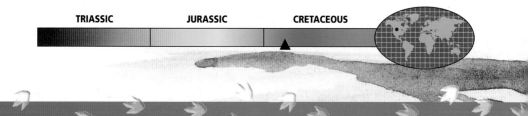

Ridged teeth

Since *Zephyrosaurus* is a small and agile dinosaur it is really skilled at zipping around. When you have no armour plating or defensive weaponry, speed is a useful way of evading predators. *Zephyrosaurus* also has the characteristic ridged cheek teeth, which help it to chew and digest the plants that it eats.

No good at perching

Zephyrosaurus is a member of the hypsilophodontidae family and, in common with its relatives, it has long fingers and toes that made some believe these dinosaurs might have lived in trees or were very good at climbing rocks. But we now know that the toes are not jointed in a way that allows dinosaurs like *Zephyrosaurus* to perch on branches.

Mistaken

Dinosaurs are sometimes discovered and named, only for palaeontologists to later realize that this type of dinosaur has already been discovered – and called something else. Here are just some of the most famous cases of mistaken identity.

Apatosaurus

Brontosaurus

Brontosaurus used to be one of the most famous dinosaurs around – even this author remembers reading about it as a child, and I'm not that old (not compared to dinosaurs, anyway). However, poor old *Brontosaurus* turned out to be the same creature as an *Apatosaurus*, and the name was consigned to history. See page 30 for more details.

Ultrasaurus

When a pair of giant back and shoulder bones were discovered during the 1980s in the USA, the remains were believed to come from a new dinosaur called *Ultrasaurus*. To confuse matters, dinosaur remains discovered in Asia at about the same time were also called *Ultrasaurus*, although it was obviously a different dinosaur. The American dinosaur was given the name *Ultrasauros* to differentiate the two discoveries. Unfortunately, it seems that neither of these

Brachiosaurus

Identity

dinosaurs are new discoveries. The Asian one was a fairly ordinary sauropod, and the American one is generally believed to be a big *Brachiosaurus*.

The whole *Ultrasaurus* episode highlights the problems that palaeontologists encounter when unearthing dinosaurs. So many dinosaurs are known only from a minimal amount of remains that confusion like this is bound to occur. Perhaps some palaeontologists have been a bit too eager to find a new species of dinosaur since to discover a new one is both exciting and prestigious.

Trachodon

If *Trachodon* is not quite an obsolete name, it is certainly of a dubious nature. When dinosaur hunter Joseph Leidy found a couple of teeth in the 1850s, he thought they were from a completely new species of dinosaur – one that he named *Trachodon*, which means 'rough tooth'.

However, in time, there were mutterings that all might not be well with *Trachodon*. The discovery of *Hadrosaurus* was enough to convince some people that the two species were in fact one and the same. Other discoveries attributed to the species were not only numerous but also turned out to be entirely different types of dinosaurs. Even the two teeth first discovered are not cast-iron proof, as they don't even come from identical species let alone the same creature's mouth.

Since one of the teeth may yet belong to a new dinosaur, the name *Trachodon* has been kept on ice, in case any more evidence backs up the claim that such a dinosaur existed.

Hadrosaurus

Discovery

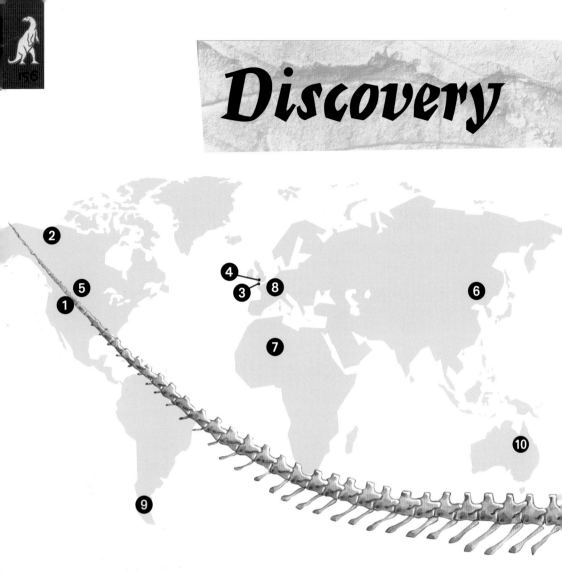

Dinosaurs have been discovered on every continent on earth, although some areas have a larger concentration of finds than others. This may indicate either the amount of time spent excavating the fossil beds (areas with a high concentration of fossils) or the number of dinosaurs that lived in a particular area.

Baryonyx claw

Sites

The following is just a selection of famous dinosaur sites from around the globe:

1 Dinosaur National Monument, Utah, USA

2 Dinosaur Provincial Park, Alberta, Canada

3 Isle of Wight, UK

4 Jurassic Coast, Devon, UK

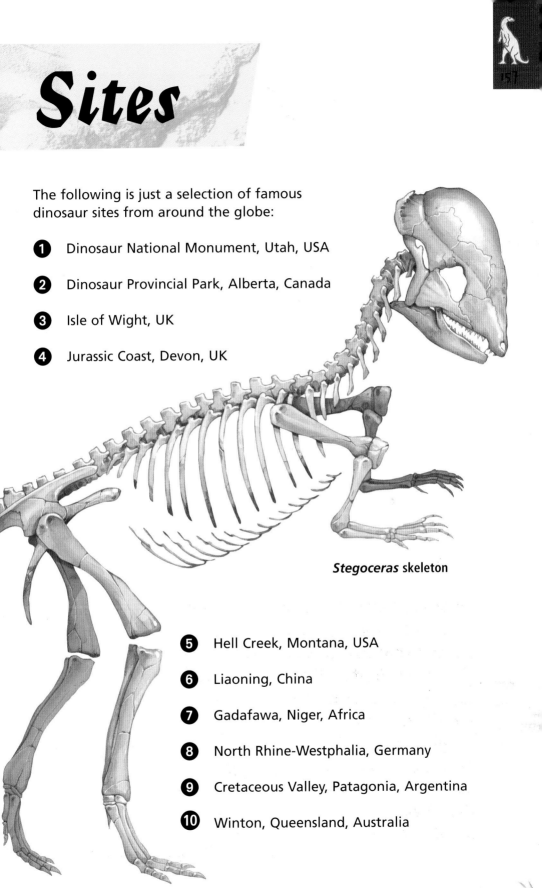

Stegoceras skeleton

5 Hell Creek, Montana, USA

6 Liaoning, China

7 Gadafawa, Niger, Africa

8 North Rhine-Westphalia, Germany

9 Cretaceous Valley, Patagonia, Argentina

10 Winton, Queensland, Australia

Dino Hunting

Looking for fossils can be long, hard and frustrating work. Many people find nothing, not even a two-a-penny sea creature, much less a dinosaur. Even the professionals return empty-handed some of the time. The idea, however, that they might find something special is what keeps the enthusiasts going and, occasionally, someone strikes lucky.

The tools you need depend on where you're looking. If you're fossil hunting somewhere like the Jurassic Coast on the Devon coastline in England, you might not need any equipment. There, fossils can literally fall out of the cliffs as they become exposed by the elements. All you need is a keen sense of sight and a stroke of luck.

The most basic tools for fossil hunting are a small pick hammer, some protective goggles and a container to keep your finds in, so that they won't get bashed about.

Homalocephale

Anchisaurus

Here are a few basic guidelines to follow:

❶ Please be careful! Often fossils turn up in pretty dangerous places, such as in quarries or on cliff edges. If you're out hunting by the sea, keep an eye on the tide – helicopter rescues are an expensive business, so don't waste their money by taking silly risks. If possible, work in pairs.

Also, make sure that people at home or back at base camp know where you are, and be sure to inform them of any change of plan or situation.

❷ If you're going to look for fossils on private property, get permission first. Some places, such as quarries, are just too dangerous – even for the professionals.

❸ If you find anything big, tell a museum. You never know, you may have found something really important! If you have, it's vital that trained palaeontologists get to the site. They will ensure that nothing is lost or damaged, and they need to document the site in minute detail to help piece the dinosaur together again. If you really have found something new, they may even name it after you!

Archaeopteryx

Further Information

A selection of great museums from around the world:

- Cleveland-Lloyd Dinosaur Quarry, Utah, USA
- Dinosaur Farm Museum, Isle of Wight, UK
- Dinosaur Isle, Isle of Wight, UK
- Museum of Natural History, Berlin, Germany
- National Dinosaur Museum, Canberra, Australia
- National Museum of Natural History, Washington, USA
- Natural History Museum, London, UK
- Royal Tyrell Museum, Drumheller, Alberta, Canada
- The Field Museum, Chicago, USA
- Wyoming Dinosaur Center, Thermopolis, USA

Useful web sites:

http://www.dinodictionary.com/

http://www.dinoruss.org/

http://www.dinosauria.com/

http://www.enchantedlearning.com/subjects/dinosaurs/

http://www.nhm.ac.uk/visit-us/galleries/life-galleries/dinosaurs/

http://www.nmnh.si.edu/paleo/dino/index.html

http://www.palaeos.com/Mesozoic/Mesozoic.htm

http://www.tyrrellmuseum.com/